Additional Praise for
THE HAUNT OF GRACE

"*The Haunt of Grace* is up close and personal—about the speaker, and about us. We know we're being grabbed. But I like the full pack of Loder's Hounds of Heaven at my heels: wit, poetry, language, challenge, acute observation, emotion."
> —David Ogston, Parish Minister, St. John's Kirk of Perth,
> Scotland; Author of *White Stone Country*

"Loder's words, frank, compassionate and personal, call to us through the wilderness of modernity; they help us recognize signs of the transcendent and gain our bearings again."
> —Dr. Bob Edgar, General Secretary, The National Council of
> the Churches of Christ in the USA

"Ted Loder has been a beacon for a whole generation ... he has shown us how to combine creativity and social witness ... and fired our imaginations. *The Haunt of Grace* reveals the spirit behind this lifelong witness and shares the joy—and heartache—that lie at its generous and ever-hopeful heart."
> —J. Barrie Shepherd, Minister Emeritus,
> The First Presbyterian Church in the City of New York;
> Author of a dozen books of poetry and meditation

"In our largely secular country, Ted Loder's *The Haunt of Grace* teaches us how to see God's footprints in everyday occurrences and hear God's whispers for social justice and forgiveness in the faces we pass daily. Loder's words illuminate God's mystery and give us courage to surrender to it."
> —Caryn McTighe Musil, Vice President, Diversity, Equity,
> and Global Initiatives, Association of American Colleges
> and Universities, Washington, D.C.

Praise for Ted Loder

"[Loder] liberates the imagination to new experiences of God, grace, and the stuff of life."
—*Sojourners*

"[Loder] puts into words so much of what [we've] longed to say. It is his creativity, blended with penetrating honesty and unexpected humor, that lifts [his writing] out of the ordinary."
—*St. Anthony Messenger*

"[Loder] compels readers to level with themselves about some of the most intimately delicate areas of human life. To read Loder's writing is to look with penetrating honesty into one's own personality, relationship with God, and need for neighbor."
—Dr. William Muehl, Yale Divinity School

"[Loder offers] a gift of evocative images which name the things that we dread, confirm us in hope, and add color to our vision of God."
—Dr. John W. Vannorsdall, Former Chaplain, Yale University; President Emeritus, Lutheran Seminary, Philadelphia

"A creative and prophetic poet who will not stay in the pulpit."
—Father W. Paul Jones, Author of *A Season in the Desert* and *A Table in the Desert*

"Loder's [words] are a lantern to illumine the wonders, terrors, and miracles of our passing days."
—Rev. William Sloane Coffin, Pastor Emeritus, Riverside Church, New York

"Loder helps us to stretch our experiences, our emotions, and our imaginations just a little bit more."
—Rev. William H. Gray, III, Senior Pastor, Bright Hope Baptist Church; President/CEO, United Negro College Fund

"I know no one else who so movingly and honestly brings us before God in [words] that touch the personal and the social dimensions of our lives."
—Tex Sample, Robert B. and Kathleen Professor Emeritus of Church and Society, Saint Paul School of Theology

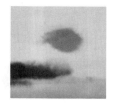

The Haunt of Grace

Responses to the Mystery of God's Presence

Ted Loder

Innisfree
Press, Inc.

A call to the
deep heart's core

Also by Ted Loder:
Guerrillas of Grace: Prayers for the Battle
My Heart in My Mouth: Prayers for Our Lives
Tracks in the Straw: Tales Spun from the Manger
Wrestling the Light: Ache and Awe in the Human-Divine Struggle

Published by Innisfree Press, Inc.
136 Roumfort Road
Philadelphia, PA 19119-1632
Visit our website at www.InnisfreePress.com.

Cover image by Sara Steele, Philadelphia, PA.
"Painting for a Winter Baby"
Collection of the Pinkerson-Feldman Family
© 1992 by Sara Steele. All Rights Reserved.

Cover design by Hugh Duffy, PhD Design, Carneys Point, NJ.

Library of Congress Cataloging-in-Publication Data
Loder, Ted, date.
The haunt of grace : responses to the mystery of God's presence / Ted Loder.
p. cm.
Includes bibliographical references.
ISBN 1-880913-57-7
1. Christian life—Methodist authors. 2. United Methodist Church (U.S.)—
Sermons. 3. Sermons, American—21st century. I. Title.
BV4501.3 .L63 2002
248.4'876—dc21
2002027559

To

Dwight E. Loder

Pastor   Educator   Bishop

A man of family, faith, hope, humor.

A model of compassion, humility, courage.

Younger Brother of my Father.

Like an Older Brother to me.

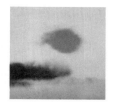

Contents

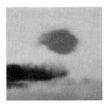

Acknowledgments

This book has emerged from a lifetime, forty-five years of which have been in the professional ministry of the United Methodist Church, thirty-eight of them as Senior Pastor of the First United Methodist Church of Germantown (FUMCOG) in Philadelphia. Of course that congregation of remarkable persons who first heard these pieces as sermons live between the lines of this book. I wish I could name each of them personally but . . .

So my staff colleagues at FUMCOG also live between these lines, including the directors of music and the organists. Each of these professional men and women contributed in different but significant ways to my life and my faith. I am particularly indebted to the first in that long line, Robert A. Raines, who surely prompted by nothing less that the haunt of grace, welcomed and endured me as a co-pastor, and in that arrangement of blessing and frustration, taught me much that remains bone deep in me. He is an old and dear friend.

My other colleagues deserve mention by name, but I refrain and trust they will know deeper than words the enormity of their gifts to me and my growth as a human being and pastor. But I must mention the last in that long line, Dr. Ann Marie Donohue, an unordained person whose gifts and spirit are singularly impressive and who has instructed, challenged, supported, and befriended me in ways that were free of clerical constraint and exceedingly beneficial to me because of it.

The foremost person I want to acknowledge is my wife and best friend, Dr. Janet I. Filing, whose insistence on the congruity of faith and life, honesty and love, hard patches and hope, direct address and quiet support, vulnerability and toughness, fragility and courage, and her prophetic stance in insisting that to love your enemies does not mean to be afraid to make them, have not only informed my life but helped transform it. In ways, this book is as much hers as mine.

What I owe to my children, now adults and parents themselves, is beyond all telling of it. Each of them—Mark, David, Karen, Thomas—has taught me more about life than I ever would have thought possible. I only hope I have taught them something about love, for they are always in my heart, however falteringly my heart is expressed in my being a father. But they have helped to take me to places that are evident in this book, and we have become closer in honest love than we might have been had we not gone there together. I rejoice and am glad in them. And in their spouses, Nadya, Steve, Amina, and children, my grandchildren, Daniel, the newest, Aaron, Lyle, Jacob, Julya, Kyle, Marek, Amanda. The revelations go on. I am also blessed by Jan's sons, Christopher and Jonathan, their wives, Valery and Hilary, and little granddaughter, Hoshaiah.

It is also time for me to acknowledge and thank Doris, the woman with whom I shared a marriage and a divorce. She is the mother of our four remarkable children and in that capacity loved, nurtured, and influenced them in good and abiding ways, and so blessed me as well. Her superb talent as a musician and her delight in her music enriched my life and that of our family, and her intelligence, her dauntless confidence, and her friendly spirit were gifts to me and a legacy to our children. The lengthy crisis of our failure in marriage deepened my self-awareness, my compassion, my re-formation as a person, and my experience of the long-suffering patience involved in giving and seeking forgiveness. Doris made important and significant contributions to my life and to my sensitivity—sometimes painful sensitivity—to the haunt of grace, which may be particularly evident in one of the responses in this book.

I am indebted to some special friends whose influence is writ large on the ensuing pages. I dare, in friendship, to name them by their first names, hoping they are good enough friends that they will forgive thoughtless but unintentional omissions. Friends know who they are without being named anyway. Still, thank you, Barbara, David, Ed, Rick, Herb, Joan, Bob, Bill, John, Kenneth, Carl, Calvin, Sheila, Harvey, Linda, Wayne, English, Sue, Doug, Austin, Ernie, Maury, Dan, Edith, Ted, Amy, Sam, Marion. That's more friends than anyone has any right to have, and perhaps I've been presumptuous to claim them as such. Some may even want to remove their names from the roll. However, they do so at their own peril.

It would be impossible to acknowledge the many teachers, preachers, poets, writers, and artists who have so profoundly shaped my own thinking, perceiving, and writing, but not to acknowledge them at all would be to claim far more for myself than is my due. I would be reduced to poverty and stupidity without their gifts to me, and to us all. At the same time, however, I hold no one but myself responsible for the limitations and flaws of this book.

Finally, I gladly acknowledge my editor and publisher, Marcia Broucek. This is not a pro forma acknowledgment but a heartfelt one. In the course of putting this book together, I broke five ribs. Marcia's patience and compassion in caring for me as a friend was far beyond any duty she had as an editor or publisher. But in that professional role, she has also been consistently patient, helpfully critical yet affirming, understanding of an author's outbursts of stubborn resistance and egomaniacal insistence, while quietly containing the damage such might have done to the work. Though this book is not her doing, it would not have been done without her.

I wish a special haunting of all of the persons, named and unnamed, who have touched this work in any way.

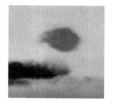

Introduction

Where I'm Coming From . . . Where I'm Headed

We live in a society that is increasingly rich in information and poor in reflection. The relative ease and speed by which we access facts and data is astounding, if not overwhelming. We can learn quickly more about any subject than we can assimilate, let alone thoughtfully interpret.

As a result, our lives are changed almost without our consent or intent. We're afflicted with near-terminal busyness. We know more but are less wise. We prefer to get information in sound bites even though the result is a sound-bite-size life. We assume love, marriage, and parenting are about perfectible techniques of manipulation rather than the faltering processes of human relationships. We consider life to consist essentially of what can be added and subtracted, touched and measured, bought and sold, managed and controlled.

Thus we are seduced into believing there are treatments for every disease and dis-ease, solutions for every problem, someone to blame (and sue) for any glitch in a process that results in a heart-rending outcome, teachable steps to follow in achieving any goal. We conclude that enough quantity equals quality, simplicity is truer than complexity, certainty is more compelling than uncertainty no matter the issue involved, knowledge is the road to wealth, power guarantees security, that Machiavelli, the Prince of Cunning, can out wrestle Beelzebub, the Prince of Darkness.

So the major change is inside each of us, in our attitudes, perceptions, and understanding of ourselves and the world. The meaning of life is reduced to whatever discovery, gimmick, promise, or advantage science, technology, the market, or privileged American citizenship pitches to us. Our self-assessment is that we are fairly predictable conglomerations of DNA, cells, chemical interactions, electrical charges, programmed impulses, and mental equipment akin to a computer—and, for most of us, a frustratingly slow one.

What is lost in all that is time and inclination to reflect, as well as the value and purpose of such reflection. What is lost is honest self-awareness, a sense of worth not defined by status, and an inclusive respect for the worth of others. What is lost is the call and the claim of any force, activity, being, or purpose that transcends the muddle of a life that is fundamentally directionless, however well informed. What is lost is the sense of a moral vision or intentional ethical action in response to that transcendence, as well as the experience of freedom and exhilaration in risking a life beyond the trite counsel of the pragmatic or safe or successful.

This book is an attempt to address those losses. Granted, to make that point, I have probably overstated the case a bit. In fact, I do not intend to demean or dismiss our contemporary world or belittle our lives in it, though I do have a "lover's quarrel" with much of both. Rather, I intend to suggest that our lives and the world are more layered, more profoundly interwoven with dimensions than we often realize. My contention is that we are haunted by transcendence at every turn, that our lives and the world are shot through with meaning and possibilities that outrun those for which, to our great deprivation, we too often settle.

No matter what the feel and thrust of every "present age," there is in all of them a great mystery about each and every life, and about the world they inhabit, including ours, and this one. Who can begin to describe or account for the incredible twists and turns, decisions and hunches, chances, influences, happenings and non-happenings, meetings and misses, losses and gains, betrayals and fidelities, triumphs and failures, the variety of people who intersected and redirected our lives—all that was involved in getting us to this moment and this place with the people who share our lives now?

Who can explain how the world has survived all the wars, plagues, epidemics, enmities, exploitations, pollution of resources and social processes, terrible misjudgments, pogroms, holocausts, bilkings, corruptions, and yet generated such incredible poetry, art, music, literature, such wondrous cultures, episodes of saintliness, movements of justice, struggles for freedom, for healing, for peace, such experiences of love and sacrifice and joy?

Surely mystery is an essential ingredient, if not *the* essential of our common life and this earth in which we are all rooted. By mystery I do not mean the vast oceans of knowledge in which we have not *yet* swum or not *yet* mapped. By mystery I mean the infinite depths of being that we can *never* plumb, never know, never exhaust, given the limits of our mortality, our finitude, our creatureliness.

Our inherent sense of mystery is in our irrepressible longing for something we cannot name but intensely miss. We are afflicted, or blessed, with a kind of insistent, cosmic homesickness. It comes in moments of awe and wonder at starlight or twilight, or a child's birth and unfolding, or the quiet peacefulness in an old woman's face, the surpassing lift of music, a pause of self-recognition in Shakespeare, or the opening of the world in a line of poetry.

The longing, the homesickness, comes in the midnight sense that we are not what we most want to be, or in the gnaw of guilt for having been or done what we know is less or other than we ought and most deeply desire. It comes in the twinge of melancholy following moments of intimacy or gladness or satisfaction which, by their fleeting nature, leave us grateful and yet strangely lonely and vaguely dissatisfied. It comes in the surge of hope in the midst of grief, or a giggle in the sudden awareness of our shared foolishness. Our experience of mystery comes in all the variations of our longing for something better, something different, deeper, more abiding than we know and have only glimpses and inklings of in our life in this world. Our experience of mystery is what Augustine called the restlessness of our hearts until they find their rest in God.

I share Augustine's view. My belief, too, is that the mystery we experience is not reducible to the capriciousness of chance or the blind fortunes of coincidence. I believe the mystery is intentional: It intends our good, our redemption. I believe it is gracious: It grants us and all the creatures of the cosmos freedom because that's what love risks doing. I believe it is holy: It makes all of creation sacred and infuses it with meaning. I believe it is personal: It suffers with us and for us, sustains us, enters into a dynamic relationship with us in which our decisions and actions are taken seriously and responded to with healing, new possibilities, and a shared, responsible creativity in the ongoing shaping of life.

It is obvious that none of what I believe can be proved, *either way*. It is a choice, profoundly personal, yet profoundly communal. It is communal because none of us creates the choice; it is offered to us by life itself and through a faith community going back centuries. It is personal because it is ours to make as free persons, to make not just once but as a daily plebiscite.

I continue to choose to understand the mystery this way not because I can make sense of it entirely but because it makes sense of me and of life as nothing else does. I gladly yet humbly confess it is a Christian way. H. Richard Niebuhr was a profound professor and presence at Yale Divinity School. Rather than indoctrinate us with a theology, Niebuhr taught us to think theologically. It was a great gift, as was his affirmation that Jesus Christ was the unique but not exclusive revelation of God. Unique—enough to be held by and to hold on to. Not exclusive—a liberating humility and openness to God's ongoing presence in the world. That has been the compass, or North Star, by which I have navigated in the world.

Charlotte Brontë reportedly said that her Christian faith was for her like wine was in water. It changed the color of her mind. Couple that with H. Richard Niebuhr, and it helps define me and this book. My faith is like wine coloring my thinking, the way I perceive the world, life, myself. To me, faith is a dynamic process such as Niebuhr and Brontë describe more than it is assent to a system of doctrines or an institution of religious practices, though these may, and at their best do, help guide and nurture faith, not conceiving it but sometimes midwifing it.

That's the case because the mystery at the heart of faith, the mystery we can choose because it chooses us first, cannot be squeezed into the shopping bags of our finite thoughts and institutions. Those thoughts, practices, convictions, and the shared actions they generate, can point to a transcendent Presence beyond those thoughts and practices. They can express a relationship with the grace of the mystery to which communities of faith try to witness. And yet, unfortunately, those thoughts, practices, convictions, and actions can too often do the opposite—as many of us have experienced, so I don't need to elaborate. Mostly the thoughts, practices, convictions, and actions of faith communities, including those I served, do a little of both nurturing and stunting. That is why the community of faith itself needs to engage in an ongoing and constant dynamic of reformation. That is my conviction, and it has been—and is—my commitment. We human beings and people of faith need to risk responding in relevant, honest, new, and faithful ways to the mystery that won't leave us alone.

So my belief is captured in the title of this book. We are haunted by grace. We are invited, urged, perhaps compelled, to respond to that haunt. Compelled, since not to respond is itself a choice and response, and not to be aware of the haunt, even dimly, is also a choice and a response, however impoverishing. What this book presents are responses of faith to the haunt of grace. In their original form, these pieces were sermons. In some instances they have been slightly expanded, and all have been at least somewhat reworked.

It seems accurate to call them responses rather than sermons, because, even in the form of sermons they were responses to the haunt of grace, the mystery of God's presence in our world and our lives.

In every case, these responses reflect my belief that the world of faith, or religion, or the Bible is not separable from the world of our present experience, the world of science, reason, practicality, art, invention, day-to-day commerce—what is commonly referred to as the "real world." Rather, I believe that to think or speak clearly and convincingly of either the world of faith or the world of our contemporary life requires us to think and talk of both at the same time. We cannot plausibly deny either of them. We need not separate them and discuss them as different realms of our existence. We don't have to drag one world to the other to illustrate or dispute either. We have the more difficult but rewarding task of discerning that the two infuse each other, uniquely but not exclusively, like wine colors water without demolishing the qualities of either.

The challenge has always been to discern and interpret the relevance of the world perceived in faith to the world experienced in our life in this world of time and events. It is to recognize, if only dimly and tentatively, the eternal haunt of grace in our everyday lives.

The challenge is to use our imagination as one of our critical human faculties, like mind or heart or spirit. It is to use our imagination in the way Richard Feynman, Nobel Laureate in Physics, described it, and I keep going back to in my thinking and faith. He said that imagination is ". . . stretched to the utmost . . . just to comprehend those things that really are there."

I have tried in this book, as in all my preaching and in my life, to use my imagination in that way, which I believe is a way of faith, integrity, and authenticity. I have used it in interpreting Scripture as well as life and the events and challenges of the world we're placed in and for which, in some sense, we are responsible. I have used my imagination in these responses to the haunt of grace hoping they will invite others to use their imaginations in ways that are authentic and stretching for them.

My intent, and my prayer, then, is that this book may honestly reflect my own continuing, partially successful struggle—and that of the community of faith I served—to live more fully, freely, creatively, and joyfully in relationship to the haunt of grace, and that it may provide an opening to others to join that struggle as well.

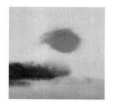

Sweaty Praise

Luke 12:22-32
Romans 8:31-39

Author E. B. White put it this way: "If the world were merely seductive, that would be easy. If it were merely challenging, that would be no problem. But I arise in the morning torn between a desire to improve the world and a desire to enjoy the world. This makes it hard to plan the day"[1] . . . or anything else, we might add.

Nevertheless, that's our common dilemma. It's a bind intensified by the terrible events of September 11th. Since then, we're torn between throwing our arms around those most precious to us, hunkering down to enjoy what we can and praying for the Department of Homeland Security, or throwing our arms around the torn, trembling world and trying to save it. We're in graduate school majoring in "dilemma." When we're bent on enjoying the world, we begin to feel guilty and anxious. When we're bent on improving the world, we begin to feel self-righteous and angry. How do we get out of that bind?

Jesus tries to tell us: "Do not worry about your life . . . Consider the ravens: they neither sow nor reap . . . and yet God feeds them . . . Consider the lilies . . . they neither toil nor spin; yet . . . Solomon in all his glory was not clothed like one of these . . ." Then he adds the rest of it: "Strive for [God's] kingdom."

The point is that God doesn't intend us to *either* improve the world *or* enjoy the world. God intends us to do *both*. Praise is the way we keep our balance between the two. Gratitude keeps us clear that not only do our gifts and our challenges come from God, but that our gifts and our challenges are essentially one and the same. The thrust of Jesus' words is that gratitude is the engine of moral action.

Without gratitude, our enjoyment of the world shrinks into cramped self-indulgence and the unscratchable itch of never having enough. And without gratitude, our efforts to improve the world degenerate into whining self-pity, anger, and frustration over the burden of our supposed moral superiority that others refuse to acknowledge.

So poet Rainer Maria Rilke points us in the right direction when he says, "The more the soul praises, the stronger it grows." Rilke is suggesting that praise is about the condition of our soul, not the circumstances of our days. Gratitude strengthens our soul by focusing on what matters.

Writer Nancy Mairs puts it in a stunning way: "Thanks to multiple sclerosis, one thing after another has been wrenched from my life—dancing, driving, walking, working—and I have learned neither to yearn after them nor to dread further deprivation, but to attend to what I have."

Thanks to multiple sclerosis? Yes, because that's how she learned the essential lesson of thanksgiving, namely ". . . to attend to what I have"!

"Consider the ravens . . . Consider the lilies . . ."

I confess that I'm not always good at being thankful. But I keep learning. I'll never forget the evening I went to a large bookstore where I was scheduled to autograph my most recent book. I fervently hoped there would be a long line of people waiting for me to sign their books. Three people showed up, and two were family.

I felt humiliated and sorry for myself. When I went to bed I couldn't sleep. About three A.M. I got up, paced, and prayed awhile. Then I started to write. You may recognize yourself in it:

What's enough? Countless times I've watched the sun rise like God's tender mercy to gently lift the dark blanket from the earth, and countless more times I've watched the sun set in such a splendiferous farewell that it must reflect the fringe on God's robe. I've seen the sky define blue and endless. I've watched rivers run to the sea, full as life runs to God. I've felt the sea roll in on the eternal note of mystery and assurance.

I've scratched the ears of dogs, laughed at the ballet of cats. I've heard the cry and gurgle of the newborn, played with children, rocked with grandmothers, learned from hundreds of teachers, some of them homeless, poor, and uneducated. I've been enlarged ten times squared by writers from Shakespeare to Toni Morrison, and yet countless other storytellers, some in delis and diners, taverns and buses, churches, curb sides and prison cells.

I have tasted bread and wine, hot dogs and caviar, somehow in the alchemy of need and gift and joy, all made holy as God's own overflowing banquet. I've been loved and forgiven beyond all deserving, and all breath to tell of it, by family and friends and God.

I've been shaken, changed, and blessed a thousand times—and still—by the prophets, and by Christ. I've felt the touch of God, each time before I realized that's what it was. I've been shrunk and stretched at the same time by the scatter of stars and found North in one of them. I've experienced the loneliness of freedom and being human and having hard choices. I've known the thrill of small triumphs, the instruction of painful defeats, and so the amazement of being part of the incredible human pilgrimage from Adam and Eve to the twenty-first century. I've shared in the cantankerous yet remarkable family of faith called the church. I'm conscious of being conscious and alive. And all that's just for starters.

How much does it take to praise God? I have a couple of trips around the Milky Way past enough for that, no matter if I never receive another thing. So I best get on with it . . . and praise God that I can.[2]

Would your list be very different from mine? Probably not. Gratitude strengthens the soul by focusing it. Because Jesus was focused on God, he was free to live in the world with daring and delight while others were stuck in their security and image issues like a swarm of killjoys.

So, yes, gratitude! Gratitude even in midst of fallout from 9/11's horrific loss from terrorism and the terrible collateral loss when we struck back at the terrorists in Afghanistan. Attend to what we have.

We all recall clearly those first pictures of dust-choked survivors running from the devastation as the World Trade Center towers collapsed. Then the images and stories of people running toward the devastated, running to meet them with open arms, open hearts, open hands, bearing gifts of prayer, time, money, blood, life itself. Then finally something deep in us somehow trusting that God was also running to that breach, that God's heart was breaking along with ours—and more, that God's hold on those who were dead and dying was tightening even as ours was inevitably loosening.

So we were made brave to go on with all the love we could muster, not only for those dearest to our hearts but also for the victims and families whose names we knew not except that they are our brothers and sisters. Perhaps we will come one day to a time when we'll realize that the victims of our war against terrorism are also our brothers and sisters. Let us pray for our enemies, as Jesus taught us to do, lest we become just like them.

Attend to what we have. *"Consider the ravens . . . Consider the lilies . . ."* It's about gratitude because this is God's world, and it is laced with God's grace. Praise is about the love we are in, always and everywhere.

Then out of gratitude comes this larger call: *"Strive for God's kingdom . . ."* There's the bristle of vitality and the glisten of sweaty gladness about that summons. *"Strive for God's kingdom."* Strive, because there's nothing easy or sentimental about it. Sooner or later, we discover that enjoyment of the world is not enough for us, or for the world. God wants more for us and from us, and so do we.

"Strive . . ." The word rightly suggests there are blisters and bruises in it. Why? Because the love of God in Christ Jesus is not meek or limited merely to lilies and larks. Look at the biblical witness where the hard, healing truth is that God defines love, not the other way around, as we often assume. Look at the prophets. Look at Jesus confronting the power brokers and hypocrites. Look at the cross. God defines love.

Consider these powerful words of St. Paul, always in the present tense:

> Who will separate us from the love of Christ? Will hardship, or distress, or persecution, or famine, or nakedness, or peril, or sword? . . . No, in all these things we are more than conquerors through him who loved us. For I am convinced that neither death nor life, nor angels, nor rulers, nor things present, nor things to come, nor powers, nor height, nor depth, nor anything else in all creation, will be able to separate us from the love of God in Christ Jesus our Lord.

What's so amazing about these words is not just that nothing is able to separate us from the love of God, though that's amazing enough. But the wonder of it runs deeper. The wonder is, that since *nothing* can separate us from the love of God, then *everything* links us to that love: hardship, peril, distress, failure, things present, things to come, everything in life and death and the whole of creation.

Now that's the deepest mystery of God's love. I do not pretend to understand it. Yet isn't that our experience? Isn't that what we are learning in the terrible turbulence whipped up by terrorism? Isn't that what the cross is about, and the empty tomb? That's what this love we're in is about. Nothing separates, everything links us to the love of God in Christ Jesus. That's the love we're in!

It is also what the love in us is about as well, or can be. A few years ago a feature in the Sunday *Philadelphia Inquirer* called the church I served "The Odd Ball Church." It wasn't a slur. The reporter got it just right. What else would a gathering of Christians be but at least a little odd—at odds with the counsels of timidity and security, comfort and consumption; at odds with the ways of injustice, exploitation and discrimination; at odds with the stifling ways of institutional self-serving and pompous self-righteousness and the idolatry of inflated nationalism? What else but odd would any group be that took Christ seriously, that tried to strive for God's kingdom? If we weren't odd enough to have a lovers' quarrel with the world, we wouldn't be anything that mattered much.

Strive! Be odd! That involves taking risks. It means taking on controversial issues because they're the ones that matter: relational justice, racial justice, gender justice, environmental justice, confronting and closing the gap between rich and poor, between our world and the Third World.

Being odd means striving to be creative and courageous in reaching out to all God's people: to those who sit next to us on the train or bus, to those sitting in the houses and offices around to us, reaching out to those sitting on the grates and in the ghettos of our cities and towns. Reaching out to homosexuals, to different political and religious orientations, different nationalities. Reaching out to kids on drugs, to kids who out of some awful emptiness do acts of terrible violence, to kids around the world dying of starvation and curable diseases. Reaching out to people trapped in the oppression of poverty and exploitation and despair and so are fodder for fanaticism and terrorism. To take Christ seriously is be at least a little odd, thank God.

"I am convinced that . . . {nothing} in all creation will be able to separate us from the love of God in Christ Jesus our Lord." That's the heart of the freedom that enables us to let go of what is familiar and comfortable and strive for God's kingdom. It is the freedom to not be afraid of uncertainty, or of tomorrow.

Now we are cheek-by-jowl with the frightening challenge of terrorism. Surely a limited measure of military action is needed toward the terrorists. But just as surely our country's response needs to expand to become one of compassion and generosity, which will be hard for us to do unless we develop a larger vision of the kingdom we strive toward.

Nahum Barnea, a columnist with a major Israeli newspaper recently wrote, "The terrorism of suicide bombers is born of despair. There is no military solution to despair."

Barnea is right. So our response to terrorism must go beyond bombs and missiles, and just as surely the church needs to raise its voice for such a response. To begin, we need to raise our voice for our own humble self-examination. Otherwise, Reinhold Niebuhr's word will fit us too well: "The self-righteous are guilty of history's greatest cruelties. Most evil is done by good people who do not know they are not good."[3] Jesus put it starkly: "No one is good but God alone." So it is dangerously simplistic and unChristian to label others as evil and ourselves as good. Instead, we need to try to understand why others see us as evil and themselves as good lest our stated goal of wiping terrorists off the face of the earth accomplish just the opposite—creating more of them.

We need to raise our voices calling for the causes of terrorism to be addressed as well as its effects to be stemmed. More than one-third of the populations of the world's poorest countries, including Palestine, is under fifteen years old. They see a bleak future for themselves. That makes them easy recruits for suicide bombing missions. Terrorism is fed by poverty. It is fed by hunger, disease. It is fed by the despair of being marginalized, dehumanized, exploited.

Surely we're called by the time to reflect on our own profligate consumerism by which we gobble up forty percent of the world's resources. Surely we're called to reflect on and reduce our wasteful use of fossil fuel. Surely it is time to end our lip service to environmental concerns while our actions, and those of government and industry, add to its deterioration. Someone pointed out that our nation seems to build alliances only for military purposes, but what is needed now is to build an alliance to address the poverty and deprivation that generate hatred and nurture terrorism.

There is much talk that since September 11th we are living in a different world. That is only partially true. The deeper truth is that since 9/11 we have the choice to live in the world *differently*. We have the chance to find a truer place in it, a humbler place, a more compassionate place in it.

Freedom is indeed a precious gift. But freedom is more than having choices at the mall, or in the voting booth, or in the unbridled pursuit of personal pleasure. I passionately believe that our deepest longing is for the freedom Jesus spoke of, lived out, and calls us to share: the freedom not to be afraid. Even small doses of that freedom will enable us to live in the world differently.

So consider it again: *"Do not worry about your life . . . Consider the ravens . . . Consider the lilies . . . Strive for God's kingdom."* Then Jesus makes this incredible promise: *"Do not be afraid . . . for it is your Father's good pleasure to give you the kingdom."* Every day we're called to step out on that promise. The mystery is that it is in striving for the kingdom that we discover it's a gift to us.

I carry in my heart a little poem a very old woman gave me many years ago. She was nearly blind then, crippled by arthritis, a retired school teacher and quite poor, living on her small pension, much of which she gave to support causes she believed in. The poem is this:

> You say the little efforts that I make will do no good,
> They will never prevail to tip the hovering scale
> Where justice hangs in the balance.
> I don't think I ever thought they would.
> But I am prejudiced beyond debate
> In favor of my right to choose which side
> Shall feel the stubborn ounces of my weight.[4]

Over the years I have gained passion and courage and joy from those words. They hint at what striving for God's kingdom is about.

So I ask you, what side of which issue needs the stubborn ounces of your weight? What are the human needs that knock on your heart now and plead with your conscience for those ounces? How will you strive for God's kingdom? Where will you cast your ounces, not to get praise but to give it? Those are our God-given choices and our chance to be blessed.

We dare not give in to the sirens of cowardice and greed and hate and fear. Ours is to strive to heal wounds, to lift the despairing all around us. Ours is to join with God in striving to create beauty where there is ugliness, peace where there is hostility, freedom where there is oppression, new life where there are dead ends.

When Susannah Wood graduated from Radcliffe College, she gave a prayer at her baccalaureate service. The prayer included these lines: "Help us to prepare a kind of renaissance in our public and private lives. Let there be born in us a strange joy that will help us to live and to die, and to remake the soul of our time."[5]

Even so, our calling is to remake the soul of our time. Is it too much to suggest that in our time any renaissance worth the name must join the private lives of each of us to the public life of all of us, and join the life and future of this nation with the lives and futures of all the nations on this blue planet home we share? Finally, there is no "me and mine" in God's world. Remaking the soul of our time requires striving to recover the "we and the ours" of our common human destiny.

Reinhold Niebuhr once said, "We should be less concerned with the purity of our actions than with the integrity of our compromises." I'm persuaded. In this complex world we all have to make compromises, for only the fool, the tyrant, and the terrorist claim to know the ultimate will of God and the absolute truth of anything.

Yet, in this historic moment, as in all moments of life, let us not compromise our integrity and humanity. As we confront terrorism and make critical decisions in the face of the uncertainties and complexities of life, let us not compromise the faithful walk of wisdom and humility for the fearful stumble of simplistic answers and vengeful actions. Let us not compromise our courage into passivity, our creativity into conformity, our compassion into indifference, our conscience into cynicism, the deepest longing of our humanity into the bondage of comfortable but illusory security, our faith into trivial pursuits. Instead, let us *"Consider the ravens . . . Consider the lilies . . . Strive for God's kingdom."*

~

1. Recalled on E. B. White's death, in *Newsweek*, October 14, 1985.

2. Condensed from "This Wrestle Through the Night" by Ted Loder in *My Heart in My Mouth: Prayers for Our Lives* (Philadelphia: Innisfree Press, 2000), 126-31.

3. As quoted by Bob E. Patterson in *Reinhold Niebuhr: Makers of the Modern Theological Mind* (Waco, TX: Word, Inc., 1977), 89.

4. Bonaro W. Overstreet, "Stubborn Ounces," *Hands Laid Upon the Wind* (New York: W. W. Norton, 1955).

5. As quoted by Robert A. Raines in *Soundings* (New York: Harper and Row, New York, 1970), 127. Originally published as "A Commencement Prayer" by Susannah H. Wood in *The New York Times,* June 17, 1968.

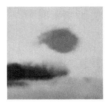

Where's Your Tattoo?

Jeremiah 31:31-34
Matthew 17:1-13

Whenever I travel, I duck into my seat on the plane or train, immediately open a book or folder of papers, screw up my best anti-social scowl, all to forestall any conversation with the person in the next seat. In fact, my idea of paradise is to have no one in the next seat.

That doesn't happen often. Usually the next seat is taken by the most talkative person traveling in my direction that day. If the person insists on talking, I am barely polite. If they ask what I do, I try never to admit I'm a clergyman. If I slip and tell them, I inevitably spend the rest of the trip squirming while being grilled on what I think, or lectured on what they know, about religion.

So, if asked what I do, I answer that I'm not at liberty to tell them. That usually silences them because they assume I'm some kind of agent for the CIA or the FBI. My position is that if people want to talk about life and death, salvation and damnation, true or false religious issues, come to my turf and get serious. Don't just casually assault me on the plane or train.

It's amazing how often God doesn't seem to agree with my position. Take the trip I made to Richmond, Virginia, not very long ago to kick off a Lenten preaching series. I was sitting there on the train waiting for it to pull out of Philadelphia's 30th

Street Station when this stylish looking guy sits down next to me. He's wearing a tailored, expensive-looking leather coat, razor-creased slacks, a cashmere sweater over a turtleneck, carrying an matching leather traveling bag and attaché case, the complete *GQ* look with an aroma of fresh lime and ocean breeze after-shave wafting about him. He's a "rainmaker" personified. My biases rocketed into orbit. I dived into my book. He dived into a computer magazine.

Half an hour later, he pulled out a portable computer and went to work on whatever it was. Good, I thought. He won't want to talk. Then, coming into Baltimore, I heard music. I looked around. It was coming from his computer. "Do you know what that is?" he asked.

"Sounds like banjos," I reflexively answered.

"It's the banjo duet from the movie *Deliverance,*" he announced. "Great movie, right? You see it?"

It was too late. I'd taken the bait and he'd hooked me. Except for his visit to the Club Car, we talked all the way to Richmond. He began by informing me of all the places he and his wife of five years had gone on vacation, including accommodations, prices, air fares, all the sights—Hawaii, Paris, Mexico, a Mediterranean cruise. My impression of him was confirmed. He asked me for ideas for their next vacation. I suggested Hoboken. Or Haiti. At least he laughed. I took that as a hopeful sign. My cargo of biases began to slip.

He said he'd been to Haiti. I was stunned. I'd been there. It's the poorest country in the Western hemisphere. I asked him why he'd gone to Haiti. He told me his wife was a native Jamaican from a poor family there. My biases jarred a little looser. He said he was trying to get his company to open a small production unit in Haiti to give people jobs at a decent wage. There was not an ounce of preening in his matter-of-fact explanation. A couple of my biases about him jettisoned into space.

He shrugged off my compliments about his efforts and went on to tell me that last year, in Hawaii, he and his wife had gotten identical tattoos but he couldn't show me where. I assured him that was okay! He volunteered that his tattoo was over his heart. So was his wife's, but he insisted that only he, her doctor, and maybe her friends in the shower at the gym would ever see it.

"That's too bad for the rest of us," I said.

He laughed again. "The tattoo is a little cross with a crown around it," he went on. "We're far from being religious fanatics or anything, but she and I thought that would be a good thing. A kind of a reminder. I mean, we're blessed and need to share that." More biases flew off into the wild blue. "You ought to get one yourself," he suggested.

"Maybe," I replied. "Someday."

As we swayed on from Washington, D.C., to Richmond, he told me about his retired parents. Just before last Thanksgiving, his mother had surgery for kidney cancer and then, just before Christmas, she had a mastectomy. She was taking Tamoxifen and seemed to be doing fine. He traveled to Richmond every couple of weeks to visit her. But he was on his way to Richmond that afternoon because the next day his father was having heart surgery. "I'm a little worried but still pretty confident," he said. "I'm sure you know that study about prayer."

He hadn't asked and I hadn't told him I was a minister. Maybe I just smell that way or something. A little suspiciously, I asked, "What study?"

He said, "The one that showed that people who are sick and are prayed for do better than sick people who don't get prayed for. Even when they don't know they're being prayed for, they do better. I'm sure that's why my mother is doing so well, and why my Dad will, too. Lots of people are praying for them, including my brother and sister and I."

I admitted I'd heard of that study.

"Impressive, isn't it?" he said.

I agreed.

When we said good-bye at the station in Richmond, I told him I'd pray for his father the next day. He said, "Thanks, Reverend." I asked him how he knew that about me. He said, "I recognized you from the brochure my parents have about the Lenten series at St. Paul's. And you really ought to think about getting a tattoo. Reminds you of things, you know? Well, God bless you." And off he waving went.

I thought about that encounter a long time. It reminded me of a poem my Scottish clergy friend, David Ogston, sent me. When I got home, I dug the poem out. It's called "Getting It Across." It's by U. A. Fanthorpe, and she's a wonderful poet. I know poems can be difficult, but this one's worth the effort. Here's a part of the poem. Jesus is speaking:

I envy Moses, who could choose
The diuturnity of stone for waymarks
Between man and Me. He broke the tablets,
Of course. I too know the easy messages
Are the ones not worth transmitting;
But he could at least carve.
The prophets too, however luckless
Their lives and instructions, inscribed on wood,
Papyrus, walls, their jaundiced oracles.

I alone must write on flesh. Not even
The congenial face of my Baptist cousin,
My crooked affinity Judas, who understands,
Men who would give me accurately to the unborn
As if I were something simple, like bread.
But Pete, with his headband stuffed with fishhooks,
His gift for rushing in where angels wouldn't,

Tom, for whom metaphor is anathema,
And James and John, who want the room at the top—
These numskulls are my medium. I called them.

I am tattooing God on their makeshift lives.
My Keystone Cops of disciples, always
Running absurdly away, or lying ineptly,
Cutting off ears and falling into the water,
These Sancho Panzas must tread my Quixote life,
Dying ridiculous and undignified,
Flayed and stoned and crucified upside down.
They are the dear, the human, the dense, for whom
My message is. That might, had I not touched them,
Have died decent and respectable upright deaths in bed.[1]

Surely, some of these wonderful images park in your memory, or your heart.

"My Keystone Cops of disciples . . . They are the dear, the human, the dense, for whom my message is . . ."

Yes, that fits us, as well as Peter, James and John who gasped after Jesus on his climb up the mountain Matthew tells us about. Those three Keystone Cop disciples schlepped along without much of a clue about why they were headed up the mountain anyway. Maybe they figured it was to get away for a rest. Or maybe just to take in the view and clear their heads. Or maybe to plan strategy. Or maybe to pray, mountain tops typically considered to be closer to God. The climb took them all day, and when they got to the top, it was midnight dark.

But what happened then caught them totally off guard—as usual. What happened is called the Transfiguration. Suddenly, on that mountain top, the shroud of darkness pulled aside and night turned dazzling. All the starlight in the heavens seemed suddenly to coalesce in Jesus, then wheel out in a thousand splendiferous directions until all around things whirled to astonished life, and the trembling air itself dropped to its knees along with the astounded disciples.

Moses and Elijah, both long dead, stepped through the veil of time and stood with Jesus, alive in the present. It linked him to these prophets and identified him as the one to lead people from bondage—not from Egypt, but from fear and sin and emptiness. Then a wave of words broke over the silence, vibrating in space like a note sung and held from some far off place: "This is my son, the Beloved . . . listen to him!" Was the voice inside them, outside, above, below, where? The disciples were frightened.

Finally, Jesus simply said to them, "Get up and do not be afraid." And when they looked, they only saw Jesus. So they got up, trusting that what had frightened them was gone.

Then they realized the darkness was not so dark anymore. What was happening was not just about the dazzling, radiant light of another world spilling over and into and out of Jesus up on that mountain. It was that the darkness of this world got several shades lighter and less frightening, including the darkness of death. That's nearly what the whole thing with Jesus is about. *"Get up and do not be afraid."*

"I am tattooing God on their makeshift lives."

Can't you just hear Jesus saying that to those dear, human, dense, Keystone Cops of disciples . . . and now to us who fit the bill just as well? And isn't that how it happens? Something like light spills over and breaks in on our makeshift lives when we don't expect it, maybe even do our best to avoid it with our excuses and doubts and arguments and biases, our anti-social scowls on the train or plane or in the living room.

A long time ago, Jeremiah the prophet heard God put it this way: "I will put my law within them, and I will write it on their hearts; and I will be their God and they shall be my people . . . they shall all know me, from the least of them to the greatest . . . for I will forgive their iniquity and remember their sin no more." Very recently, Fanthorpe the poet put words of similar weight in Jesus' mouth, and they sound right: *"I alone must write on flesh."*

And what is the needle with which the tattoo is etched, not so much *on* our hearts as *in* them? What, except the needles of the people we sit with, walk with, work with, argue with, love, or like a lot or not much at all, try to avoid but sooner or later can't. The needles of our enemies as well as people who pray for us even when we don't know it, or realize it. The needles of those who care enough to honestly challenge us with their truth as we traipse up the mountain of our week. That's how God tattoos our makeshift lives.

Sometimes we aren't even aware we're being tattooed until it occurs to us—however dimly, the next day, or week, or month, or year—that the tattoo is there in us somehow, haunting us all along in the longing that sends us traipsing wherever we go. Or in the joys that punctuate the landscape of our lives like mountain tops. Or in the stubborn hope that keeps getting us up and making us several shades less afraid. The light breaks in, for an infinite instant, transfigures us and things around us, in little ways, and sometimes large ones. In the music of a song we find ourselves humming. In the touch of a friend. In the eyes of a child. In a story that breaks open our hearts. In a praying moment when our words fade out and a sense of being heard shivers through. In a night when the starlight strikes us, too, and shushes our babble and puts our souls on their knees.

So the yuppie in the custom-made leather jacket asks, "Do you know the study that showed that people who are sick and are prayed for do better than sick people who don't get prayed for? Even when they don't know they're being prayed for, they do better." And a tattoo needle of this no-longer-quite-as-much a stranger cuts through your biases and etches a cross on your heart. It happens all the time, transfigurations like that.

I keep tucked away for rereading an issue of *Sports Illustrated* in which there was a simple story about Don Haskins, the coach of Texas Western who in 1966 put a lineup of all-black players on the floor and beat an all-white Kentucky team for the National Championship. By doing that, Haskins changed the face of college basketball forever, even though he got thousands of death threat letters as a result.

That big spill of light through Haskins was like those through Jackie Robinson and Branch Rickey in baseball, and Thurgood Marshal standing tall before Justice Warren and the Supreme Court in Brown *vs.* the Board of Education and the Court's decision to make racially separate but equal school systems illegal.

But just as important as the big thing was that Haskins stayed at that college, now called the University of Texas El Paso, for thirty-eight years and turned down more lucrative coaching positions. Now retired, he has little money. He spent most of what he had on medical care for his son, who died. But his friends say that wasn't the only thing that left Haskins in the hard scrabble. It was his generosity and compassion. Typically, every day for years, he left a ten-dollar tip for a lonely waitress in a dumpy, usually mostly empty coffee shop where he and his two assistant coaches had coffee, never more than a cup or two apiece. That was a spill of light, a transfiguration, too.

The point is simple. It's not just the big stuff, the big people, but every person we meet, every choice we make, every act we do, every word we speak that matters enormously. Those encounters are cracks through which light squeezes into this world because God is always using someone around us as needles to tattoo grace and mercy and hope and joy on our makeshift lives.

And using us to do that on the makeshift lives of others, as well. That's the rest of it. The disciples followed Jesus down from the mountain of ecstasy out into the world of need. Even so, each of us is a tattoo needle leaving some indelible mark on someone else, maybe never recognized but essential, mysteriously multiplied like loaves and fishes to feed the hunger, the longing, the needs of more others than we know. Half the message of the transfiguration of Jesus is that it is never as dark as we think it is. Never. By God, there's always enough light.

That's what those three numbskulls like us discovered up there on the mountain: Peter with fish hooks in his head band, and James and John with reservations in their pockets for rooms at the top. The midnight dark wasn't so dark after all because they could see Jesus in it. And hear him say, *"Get up and do not be afraid."* That's the gospel in miniature. And the thing to notice is that there were three of them there. Not one, alone, but three together. Eyesight improves when there is more than one pair of eyes looking and more than one life to see or reflect the light.

This Keystone Cop of a disciple knows what fear is. Do I ever! And doubt and discouragement and all the rest. But I am less afraid, less discouraged, more faithful when I am not alone, when I am with others, people I love. Faith and courage are contagious.

"You ought to get a tattoo like mine. Reminds you of things."

I should have said, "I have one. On my heart. You and countless other people in my life helped God put it there."

What does it mean to be those Christ calls to be needles to tattoo God on the makeshift lives of others? Look again at what the poet says it meant to those first disciples:

These Sancho Panzas must tread my Quixote life . . .
They are the dear, the human, the dense, for whom
My message is. That might, had I not touched them,
Have died decent and respectable upright deaths in bed.[2]

I suppose most of us will die "decent, upright deaths in bed," because the crucifixions and stonings and flayings that ended the first disciples' lives are out of style these days. Still, the point holds: Whoever those dear, human dense ones are who get the message, we are surely among them. We can take risks, go against the conventional, safe practices, work for justice, embrace and include the rejected and oppressed. We may die decent deaths, but we don't have to be so respectable in the process.

So where is your tattoo? Where is your tattoo needle? Think of your own precious children. Think of your family and friends. Think of those you work alongside, or live with in the neighborhood, or vote with, give to. Think of the welfare mothers homeless with the kids on the streets, the working poor who are not paid a living wage. Think of those burdened and dehumanized by racism, sexism, homophobia, indifference. Think of the people we dehumanize with our biases, whoever they are. God gives us strange company in our struggle.

"I am tattooing God on their makeshift lives."

We Keystone Cop, tattoo-needle people need to decide what that means for us and those for whom we are the message. The thing is, we decide every day, every hour, with everyone we meet, because it's all important. And it is never as dark as we think. Christ is in it. And so are we. As for me, then, I suspect I'll own up to what I do next time I'm asked by a fellow traveler.

"Get up and do not be afraid."

In her book *Amazing Grace*, Kathleen Norris describes how the poet Mary Oliver used this story from the life of William Blake as an epigram for her book:

> Some persons of a scientific turn were once discoursing, pompously, and to [Blake], distastefully, about the incredible distance of the planets, the length of time light takes to travel to the earth, etc. when [Blake] burst out, "Tis false! I was walking down a lane the other day, and at the end of it, I touched the sky with my stick."[3]

The poet recognized the truth. And so do we, if we pay it half a mind, half a heart. God is not far off across endless space and millennia of time. Nor is Christ or the transfiguration, or the light of eternity and the stuff of meaning and hope and joy, or the kingdom of God. The whole thing is as close as the person next to us on the train, or the plane, or the street, or in the ghetto, the barrio, the villages of the desperately poor in Africa or Afghanistan or Palestine or Haiti or Mexico, or in the violent bashing in the Middle East. As close as persons anywhere you put your finger, or your heart, on the globe of this one little planet, home of us all.

Norris, commenting on the Blake story, said she wished ". . . that Blake had lived long enough to hear quantum physicists speaking like poets . . . confirming that 'every atom of our bodies was once inside a star.' "[4] Even so, we can touch people, the stars, God, with our sticks, our hands, our hearts, our votes, our time, our money. And they can, and do, touch us back. All around, Christ is there where we don't expect him, or recognize him most of the time. Nevertheless, there he is.

"I am tattooing God on their makeshift lives."
On theirs and ours.

~

1. U. A. Fanthorpe, "Getting It Across, *Selected Poems* (London: Penguin Books Ltd. 1986), 72-73.

2. Ibid., 73.

3. Kathleen Norris, *Amazing Grace: A Vocabulary of Faith* (New York: Riverhead Books, a member of Penguin Putnam Inc., 1998), 381.

4. Ibid., 381.

In Your Face

2 Corinthians 4:1-18

Matthew Poncelet, convicted of the brutal murder of two young people, comes through the door of a prison holding cell and begins walking toward the death chamber. Among the guards and officials with Poncelet is a nun, Sister Helen Prejean, who has been his spiritual advisor during his last days on death row. For a moment Poncelet falters and slips to his knees. Helen Prejean kneels beside him. She says, "Look, I want the last thing you see in this world to be a face of love. Will you look at me when they do this thing? You look at me. I'll be the face of love for you."[1]

Poncelet looks intently at her, climbs back to his feet, and walks on toward the room where he will be put to death. Helen Prejean walks with him to the door, her hand on his shoulder. Then she sits with the witnesses on the other side of the glass window looking into the chamber.

Among the witnesses are the parents of the young woman who was viciously raped by Poncelet and his partner before she was killed, and the father of the young woman's fiancé who was murdered with her after they were dragged from their car parked on a Louisiana lover's lane. As the lethal drugs are injected into him, Poncelet and Prejean look steadily, searchingly at each other.

"I'll be the face of love for you."

The scene is in my heart, and it will stay there. It comes near the end of the movie *Dead Man Walking*, which is based on the book written by Sister Prejean about her experience.[2] It is a powerful, spiritual movie because it is fair to all sides of the story and probes so deeply into the human heart.

As Poncelet is prepared for execution and as the lethal injections begin, his eyes are on Helen Prejean and her eyes on him. There are tears in her eyes. She reaches out her hand to him in a kind of embrace. Her lips move in prayer and assurance with the words, "I love you," even as across the screen flash images of the terrible crime he committed and the faces of the two murdered young people.

How could she do that? How could she be the face of love for him in spite of so much vileness, so much hostility toward her, so much dishonesty and manipulation?

What would it mean to be a face of love in this world where there are so many faces of hate and fear and anger and arrogance? What would it mean to be a face of love in our "in-your-face" society where we are so ready to stick our accusing face in the face of anyone in our way or out of our favor? What would it mean to be a face of love for someone we consider contemptible, someone we consider utterly wrong, misguided, stupid, even inhuman and evil—all the varieties of Matthew Poncelet that shadow our days and inhabit our nightmares? What would it mean to go at life with such compassion and hope, such faith and courage, that those qualities would somehow be etched in our face?

There are some clues in 2 Corinthians. First this one, as Paul put it to the Corinthians, and to us: "We have this treasure in clay jars, so that it may be made clear that this extraordinary power belongs to God and does not come from us." Faith grasps the difference between clay jars and the treasure of grace.

The face of love begins and continues in a clear awareness of our limitations. We are all clay pots. In a basic sense faith begins with that awareness. When Sister Prejean says she will be the face of love for Poncelet, it's a statement of faith. Through the whole time of being Poncelet's spiritual advisor, Helen Prejean never acted as if she were better than he was, or that she knew more than she did. In her book she writes that, at the end, Poncelet said to her, "I thought you'd be doin' nothin' but preachin' to me, but after our first visit I saw I could just talk to you like a friend."[3]

Sister Prejean was always willing to recognize and admit her limits and mistakes without being defensive. When she first responded to the killer's request to visit and talk with him, she overlooked and ignored the victims' families. She didn't go to them as well as to the killer. But she was humble enough to learn from her mistake. When the victims' parents confronted and blamed her for forgetting them in favor of their children's killer, she admitted she was wrong and was deeply sorry for it. She began to relate to them with humility and compassion. She was always aware of her status as a clay jar.

How rare that is these days! Too many of us are more like the self-righteous Englishman in the joke where he insists he always did "what the Lord would do if He only had the facts in the matter." Or those who *know* which side God is on, which clearly is "our" side, not "their" side. Oh my, it isn't only the political and religious right who seem blind to being clay pots, it is the political and religious left and the middle as well. *All of us!* Whatever else it is, love is not arrogant or self-righteous.

Actress Susan Sarandon, who played Sister Prejean's part in the movie, said that the movie and the book were not about who deserves to die, but who deserves to kill. Absolutely accurate!

It isn't much of a stretch to take that insight to other human issues, is it? Who deserves to kill, to condemn, to dominate, to silence others, to disregard and disrespect anyone, to kill people by execution or in a hundred more subtle ways? With drugs and poverty, underfunded schools and inadequate health care, yes, but also with gossip, silence, avoidance, indifference. Who deserves to do that? Not one of us. Yet, we do all it. And that's to say nothing of killing with planes, guns, bombs, missiles.

Surely we grasp that to stand for something does not require condemning or dehumanizing those who stand for the other side. Helen Prejean opposed the death penalty, but she still listened to and had compassion for the terrible pain and profound loss of the victims' families. She understood their view of justice. That takes courage, and knowing you are a clay jar, not the treasure. Prejean talked to and sought to understand the terrible dilemmas of the prison people whose duties involved performing the execution. She constantly and passionately prayed for God's help and guidance for herself because she was aware of her weakness and limited vision. Compassion is contained in a clay jar, not a stainless-steel one.

Clay jars know they are not really better than other clay jars, no matter how poor or cracked those others might be. So they can cry for them, as the tears in Helen Prejean's eyes testified. And yet, they know as well, *"We have this treasure in clay jars . . ."* That's a response to the haunt of grace. The treasure is love, and love is always a gift. Always. It is freely given, not coerced. It is not an achievement or a reward. It is a gift, whether we receive it or share it. It haunts us at every turn of our common life. God's love is always at work in us and around us in steady but mysterious ways, so we can smile with tears in our eyes:

"I'll be the face of love for you."

~

Here is the second clue to being the face of love. In his letter to the Corinthians, and to us, Paul writes: "Since it is by God's mercy that we are engaged in this ministry, we do not lose heart." I believe the ministry Paul is talking about is the ministry of not letting discouragement keep us from persistently risking being accessible and reaching out to all people, regardless of who or what they are, as Paul did to the cantankerous Corinthians.

I know well how hard it can be to reach out, to listen to, and learn from, people who are different from us because they are of another culture, or religion, or nationality, or generation, or because they have ideas or attitudes or convictions that make us uncomfortable, even angry or frightened. Yet that is very close to the heart of what Jesus is about: God sneakily reaching out to each strange, different, fumbling, difficult one of us.

One of the striking things in *Dead Man Walking* is the courage and persistence of Helen Prejean in reaching out to people and not losing heart. She lived and worked in the worst ghetto of New Orleans. She kept reaching out to Matthew Poncelet, who was an exceedingly obnoxious man, a white supremacist, a macho braggart, a liar, a killer. She reached out to the victims' families, visited them in their homes—even when the parents of the murdered young woman assumed that her visit meant she'd come over to their side and believed Poncelet deserved to be put to death, then angrily asking her to leave when she told them she hadn't come over to their side but was there to listen and to pray with them.

Reaching out means going deep as possible with people into their pain and anger, their fear and hope, meeting them in those depths, listening, trying to understand, sharing ourselves with them. One of the sad things about our frantic busyness is how shallow our relationships become under the poverty of time. We slowly, subtly dehumanize each other, and ourselves, by reducing life to networks of functions in the service of social contacts, careers, bottom lines, goals. Our lives become a compulsive effort to make ourselves more efficient, more attractive, more successful, with better résumés—or obituaries.

Maybe we don't intend to do that, but then the issue is we don't intend *not* to hard enough. As someone said, "It's easy to slip into the current and let it carry you away." It is so easy to shrug as the fabric of society frays and pulls apart. It takes courage not to lose heart, to go against the current, to be present and accessible to each other, even when we don't feel like it.

That's why it is so important for us to pray and worship together, to reach out to each other and to God week by week. It helps us to not lose heart. Then we're renewed to reach out to people in the community around us. Reaching out is what love is, and what the church is about.

Forgive me a personal witness. After a meeting one evening, I walked with a woman to her car across Germantown Avenue from the sanctuary. After she drove off and I turned to go back toward the office, I saw four black men and two black women and a small child come out of the store there. I said hello and added, "That's a beautiful little kid you have."

In no uncertain terms, the men objected to my use of the word "kid," reminding me that it refers to a goat with hair all over it. I said "You're right. I'm sorry I said it that way because that's not what I meant. I apologize for offending you. She's a beautiful little girl."

They were not satisfied. One walked behind me as I went back across the street, then motioned for me to follow him around the corner to a darker spot on High Street. I went, with my heart beating a little faster. When we'd walked a few yards up the street where the shadows were deep, he stopped. I looked him in the eye and asked him what he wanted.

He said, "White guys don't talk to black children."

I said, "Why not?"

He pushed me and answered, "Because I said so. It's patronizing."

Maybe he could hear my heart pounding through my shirt,

but I said, "Hey, I talk to black children and black people all the time. I'm the minister of this church, and we care about all the people in this community. Including you and your friends and the little girl. I know black people have lots of reasons to distrust whites, but we're trying to do something about that. That's why I risked coming with you into this dark street."

He shoved me again and called me an unflattering name.

I said, "Look, we can fight if you insist. But you know we'll both get hurt. So you and I having a fight isn't going to do anyone any good. What's in it for you?"

I knew what was in it for him and could have told him. It was a way for him to strike back at all the prejudice and oppression and dehumanization white people have visited on black people. It was a way for him to recapture some of his manhood and perhaps gain stature in the eyes of his friends and the little girl. But for me this was between the two of us human beings.

But I asked him again, "What's in it for you?"

For a couple of heartbeats he stared off toward Germantown Avenue. The question seemed to give him pause. After a moment he looked in my face and, as if for the first time, saw past its whiteness. Then he said, "If you really care, and respect me and my friends, apologize for what you said."

I gladly repeated the apology I'd made earlier and began to walk back toward Germantown Avenue. At first he hesitated, as if we hadn't finished—and we hadn't, not with two-hundred years of justified grievance. But we had finished with that brief moment of confrontation, confession, and at least tentative reconciliation, even love. He realized that, I think, because he turned toward me, and we walked back together without a word but, I think, some mutual respect and understanding.

When we reached the Avenue in front of the church, he told the others, "He apologized." They nodded their acceptance and approval, then got in the car.

I said, "Good night, God bless you," and watched them drive away.

Was I scared? Absolutely! But not enough to back away from the risk of showing my face to this man, not enough to try to weasel out of our encounter. Something in me just had to reach out. You may have had similar experiences in your work or home or neighborhood and have hung in, reached out. More of us need to do that. Maybe it's hanging in and reaching out to people as close and critical as a spouse or child or parent or friend and working something out with them, or trying to. But surely it's hanging in and reaching out to people marginalized by prejudice, exploitation, and any kind of oppression.

Whatever else it's about, love is about reaching out and not losing heart. Will it make any difference? Yes, in my bones I trust it will. But when and where and how is God's business and takes God's own time. Our part is to respond to God's grace no matter how bad the world's news, or how hard the circumstance, or how frightening the way.

In her book Helen Prejean writes that she has become a friend of the parents of the raped and murdered girl, though they are on opposite sides of the issue of capital punishment. She was asked to visit the murdered girl's father in the hospital. She and both the father and mother laugh and talk together at meetings in the prison, which confuses the guards. And she prays regularly with the father of the murdered boy, and he sometimes gives her small gifts of money for her work.

"I'll be the face of love for you."

~

Then there is a third clue from Paul about what it means to be a face of love in the world: "We have renounced the shameful things that one hides; we refuse to practice cunning or to falsify

God's word; but by the open statement of the truth we com-
mend ourselves to the conscience of everyone in the sight of
God." Whatever else Paul is talking about, he's talking about
accountability. We stand always in the presence of God and are
accountable to God for what we are and do and say.

What is so powerful in *Dead Man Walking* is Helen
Prejean's insistence on trying to hold Matthew Poncelet accountable for what he has done. In the first days of the week before his execution, she tells Poncelet what Jesus says in the gospel
of John: "You shall know the truth and the truth will set you
free" (John 8:32). The convict likes that because he thinks it
means he will get out of prison and execution if he can get people
to believe that his insistent lies about his innocence are true. But
she means something much more profound, and at last he comes
to learn it.

Poncelet keeps insisting he didn't kill or rape anyone, that it
was his partner who went crazy on him. He keeps saying booze
and drugs made him go to lover's lane to scare people. He talks
about "Niggers," and the "evil" government, and the parents of
the victims trying to kill him. Finally, Sister Prejean tells him to
think of the girl's father: "He's never going to see his daughter
again. He's never going to hold her. He's never going to love her,
laugh with her . . . You blame [your partner]; you blame the
government; you blame drugs; you blame blacks . . . what about
Matthew Poncelet? Where's he in this story? What, is he just an
innocent? A victim?"[4]

I keep seeing myself in that scene, do you? Do we ever look
at ourselves and what we are accountable for, rather than blaming someone else, our spouse, our parents, our boss, the other
guys whoever they are, whatever group it is? Do we hold each
other accountable, or do we just slip-slide by, and let each other
slip-slide by, with simple answers to complicated issues,
knee-jerk cliches instead of honest exchange?

Love is not easy, only rewarding. C. S. Lewis once said, "We are not necessarily doubting that God will do the best for us, we are wondering how painful the best will turn out to be."[5] Often the truth is painful. Before it is good news, the gospel comes across as bad news for those of us who want to be confirmed as we are. Who was it said that God invites us to a "come-as-you-are party, but not a stay-as-you-are party." The word is "Repent." Turn around, like the Prodigal Son, and move toward God.

How? By moving toward each other, toward our prodigal brother or sister—which the original prodigal didn't do, much to the Father's dismay. Honest exchange is risky, and it is hard work. But it's what real, intimate relationships are about. It's what integrity is about. It's what love is about. It's what reconciliation and justice and peace are about, in home, community, world.

"You shall know the truth and the truth will set you free."

Helen Prejean is a strong, clear-eyed woman, not sentimental, not sugary or simplistic. She believes that every human being deserves respect. And she saw the possibilities beneath the surface swagger in Matthew Poncelet. Possibilities are what being accountable, and holding each other accountable, is really about. So on the night he dies, Poncelet finally confesses to what he had done. He cries as he does. He takes responsibility. And she says to him, "You did a terrible thing, Matt. A terrible thing. But you have a dignity now. No one can take that from you. You are a son of God, Matthew Poncelet."[6]

Poncelet smiles and sniffles, this macho killer, and says, "Nobody ever called me no son of God before. They called me a son-of-a-you-know-what a lotta times, but never no son of God."[7] And there is a look of wonder, even a kind of peace on his face.

That is what freedom is. It's rooted in trusting that we are a son or daughter of God. Freedom is not about getting whatever we want, or succeeding at whatever we do, or having lots of options to choose among. The deepest, most real freedom is being free to do what we believe is right without being paralyzed by fear of the cost. It's the freedom to love, to do justice—which is love in action—and to do it wherever God puts us, lest we muffle and distort the life in us as well as in others. It is being accountable.

"I'll be the face of love for you."

∿

And finally, this last clue from Paul. Read it carefully because it is the secret of it all: "For it is the God who said, 'Let light shine out of darkness,' who has shone in our hearts to give the light of the knowledge of the glory of God in the face of Jesus Christ."

The face of Jesus Christ. That face is all around us, when we look. We see it when we pray. We see it when we are aware of being a clay jar, yet containing a treasure. We see it when we reach out and make ourselves accessible to all the strange people like us in the world. We see it in each other's face when we pay close attention. We see it in the face of the poor, of children, of the homeless, in the face of those we count as enemies, in the face of the sick, the hungry, the prisoner.

We need to pay more attention to personal salvation, to the state of our souls. Put it this way: The gospel is not about less than personal salvation. It is not about less than intimacy with God and freedom from fear, bit by bit, and peace, step by step. Not less than that, but more. The more is how we live in the world, the character and conviction and compassion in us that comes out in our face over the time of our lives.

The gospel is God saying, "I'll be the face of love for you. Whoever you are, I am with you. Wherever you are, I am there in love for you in every face you see, in the face of creation itself. Trust me, the light in the darkness, deep as midnight though it seems." That's the haunt of grace, the response God invites us to make again and again, and always again.

At last, it comes down to this: No matter how much wattage we try to generate on our own, before love can truly shine in our face, the light of the knowledge of the glory of God in the face of Jesus Christ needs to shine in our soul, somehow, in whatever way we can let that happen.

Dead Man Walking: The title of the movie comes from the words a guard calls out as a condemned man, like Matthew Poncelet, walks to the room where he will be executed. The guard goes ahead on that final walk and calls out, "Dead man walking." In a sense—not a morbid sense but a true, even joyful one—we are all dead men walking somehow, dead women walking, because somewhere out there, in the days or months or years ahead, we will all die. We are clay jars.

Yet the most moving thing in the movie is that Sister Helen Prejean knew, deep in her nun's heart, that Matthew Poncelet, that dead man walking, was really walking toward not just death but life and amazing grace.

So are we. We are dead people walking toward more life every day, deeper life, truer life, more joyful life.

"Nobody ever called me no son of God, no daughter of God, before."

Well, someone has now. It's the gospel truth. God says to each one of us, *"I'll be the face of love for you, forever."*

~

1.   *Dead Man Walking*, written and directed by Tim Robbins (New York: PolygramFilm Productions B.V., 1996).

2.   Helen Prejean, C.S.J., *Dead Man Walking: An Eyewitness Account of the Death Penalty in the United States* (Vintage Books, A division of Random House, Inc., New York, 1994).

3.   Ibid.

4.   *Dead Man Walking.*

5.   C. S. Lewis, "29 April, 1959," *Letters of C. S. Lewis,* edited by W. H. Lewis (New York: Bles/Harcourt, 1966).

6.   *Dead Man Walking.*

7.   Ibid.

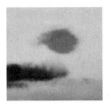

Bent Fingers

Matthew 13:31-33

Nancy was a friend, a young mother, suddenly stricken with an incurable disease. She had only a few months to live when she told me this remarkable story. She told it with a smile watered by tears. "When I was growing up," she said, "I adored my grandmother. Her name was Anna, and she lived on a farm not far from town. I loved to visit her as often as I could. When I was in seventh grade, Grandma Anna died. I was totally heartbroken and couldn't stop crying for days.

"At Grandma Anna's funeral, when no one was looking, I put a letter in her coffin. I asked her to show me a sign that she was still around and that God was real. I desperately needed comfort.

"Over the years I thought I noticed some signs of Grandma Anna's presence from time to time, but I wasn't sure, so mostly I still felt sort of vaguely forlorn. Until I was pregnant with my second child. From its conception, I was just sure the baby would be a girl. The only name I even considered for the baby was Anna. At a baby shower they asked me what we'd name it if it was a boy, and I blurted out, 'Anna.' Of course, they all laughed at me.

"The baby came two weeks late, which meant it was born on Grandma Anna's birthday. I was certain this wasn't a coincidence. And it was a girl, Anna. The first thing I noticed when they handed her to me was that her fingers were bent in a certain distinctive way. They were bent just like my Grandma Anna's fingers had been bent, an obvious, funny little quirk no one else in the family had. The family used to joke about Grandma Anna's fingers, so when little Anna turned up with those same fingers, I cried for joy. It was such a powerful, comforting sign. I knew little Anna's bent fingers were an answer to the letter I'd put in Grandma Anna's coffin."

It's an intriguing story, isn't it? How are we to understand it? Could it be that baby Anna's bent fingers were actually a sign of Grandma Anna's presence? Were they a way God touched and comforted the granddaughter who had asked for such a sign . . . or is the story about an illusion? Were little Anna's bent fingers just a coincidence, a trait explained by genetics . . . or were they a clue to something more?

Peter Gomes, preacher to Harvard University at The Memorial Church, writes, "There is in Celtic mythology the notion of 'thin places' in the universe, where the visible and invisible world come into their closest proximity."[1] Leave it to the Irish to come up with such a lovely, poetic, powerful image: thin places where the eternal world rubs close to the world of time. The Irish monks believe it is at such frontiers that God and human beings are most intimately present to each other. I love the image. All of us can name some thin places we've experienced. Gomes suggests that suffering is one, joy another, mystery yet another. We could add loss, death, birth, love, relationships of trust, sex . . . and comfort. It's as good a place as any to begin.

One Friday evening, my wife, Jan, and I were having dinner with some dear friends, and we started talking about the problems besetting our city and our society. We covered city schools, poor children, lack of funding, the poison of racism, the divisions between urban and suburban communities, the scarcity of visionary world leaders, Third World poverty, terrorism, and on and on. By the end of the evening, I was totally depressed. All night I tossed and turned, thinking about our talk. You know how that goes. It became urgent for me, as surely it's urgent for us all, to try to make sense of things like bent fingers. Are there truly thin places where God touches us with comfort and with its companion, hope?

Jesus told two little parables about thin places:

> *The kingdom of heaven is like a mustard seed that someone took and sowed in his field; it is the smallest of all the seeds, but when it is grown it is the greatest of shrubs and becomes a tree, so that the birds come and make nests in its branches.*

Then this:

> *The kingdom of heaven is like yeast that a woman took and mixed in three measures of flour until all of it was leavened.*

Would it be too great a stretch to add this parable of like kind?

> *The kingdom of God is like a little girl who puts a letter in her grandmother's coffin and years later gives birth to a baby with bent fingers as a reply.*

However you read them, Jesus' parables touch on the thin places where two worlds, two dimensions, rub together. The first, and simpler of the two dimensions, is the human side. When we hear these parables, it is easy to focus on the mustard seed and the yeast and overlook the rest of it. Yet it is critical to remember it was a man and a woman who did the small acts of planting the seed and putting the yeast in the flour.

Jesus is saying that such small acts have great consequences no one realizes at the time. Part of the mystery is that the seed and the yeast carry their own future with them, even though that future is not apparent at that moment. But the rest of the mystery is that that future depends on the small acts of the man and the woman. That is the way of God's kingdom.

Lawrence Krauss is a big-time physicist who wrote in *The New York Times* that "all the information in all the books ever written would require . . . about a million million kilobytes of storage." I've never been sure exactly what a kilobyte is, but you might, and the rest of us can take Krauss's word, that a million million of them would store more reading than we could get done in a couple of lifetimes.

Krauss goes on: "That amount [a million million kilobytes] is only one ten-millionth of a billionth of what it would take to store the pattern of a single human being, so that using currently available hard disks that would store 10 gigabytes of information each and stacking them on top of one another, you would have a pile that would reach about a third of the way to the center of the galaxy—about 10,000 light-years . . ."

If you're boggled by that, you're boggled by yourself and every person around you. The Bible is right in saying that each of us is "fearfully and wonderfully made" (Psalm 139:14)! And all those gigabytes stacked from here to Orion are not only about intelligence—or even primarily about intelligence. They're about the wondrous capacities we have for compassion, for creativity, for connecting, for relating, listening, talking, singing, capacities for sensitivity, for forgiveness and beauty, for justice and worship.

In a mysterious way, God uses us to be bearers of comfort and hope to one another. That makes each of us one of those thin places where the visible and invisible worlds rub against each other. Think of that. It is wondrous! That's what it means that we have a spirit, a soul, that we are made in God's image.

Of the four people involved in that gloomy Friday night discussion, one was a teacher in a city high school, and had been for twenty-five years; another had worked for years with senior citizens, and in job training for high-school dropouts, and now raised funds for an agency helping disabled persons; a third ran an off-campus urban semester for college students, was now director of a program for crack-addicted mothers and their children; and me, a pastor of an urban church. And all of us, parents. In the midst of ticking off all the problems, we missed ourselves. We missed each other. We missed the gratitude, the comfort in our own living. We missed how the gifts we are ripple out to others, to the city, to the kingdom. We missed our version of the clue of the bent fingers. We whizzed by the thin places each of us are.

Clearly, one point Jesus makes in the parables is that we are gifts to each other, even as the man who planted the mustard seed and the woman who mixed in the yeast were. What they did rippled out to others. In those ripples are comfort and hope. Of course, we are not perfect, or even close to it. But we are still God's gifts to each other.

Think of yourself. Think the people you touch in your work, your family, all the listening and responding and supporting and caring you do, and all others do for you. We are a thin place with and for each other.

When our Christian brother Cardinal Joseph Bernadin of Chicago died a few years ago, it was a great loss for all of us. I didn't agree with everything this outstanding Roman Catholic leader did or stood for, but he was a light in the darkness, a builder of bridges between factions in the Catholic Church, and between that church and the Protestant Church. Cardinal Joseph, as he liked to be called, battled for economic justice, for disarmament, for the poor, for the end of capital punishment.

Cardinal Bernadin knew for over a year that he was dying of pancreatic cancer, but he served his people with grace until the end. At a time when you would think he needed comfort and hope the most, he gave comfort and hope the most. That's how, in the mysterious exchange of grace, he got comfort and hope. Bernadin described his fatal illness as "God's special gift to me at this particular moment in my life. As a person of faith, I see death as a friend, as the transition from earthly life to life eternal." The Cardinal was a thin place, a bent finger. So are we all, or so can we be, if we trust and express the gift God creates us to be.

One last thing about the human side of the thin places. It has to do with the image of the small seed growing into a great bush so *"the birds come and make nests in its branches,"* and the image of the yeast raising bread for hungry people. The images are of inclusion. All creatures are included, even each of us. Even those we ignore or try to exclude, or others try to exclude. There is comfort and hope in that as well.

Peter Gomes points to where thin places are likely to be found. He writes, "Where then is hope to be found among people? Where the sufferings have been greatest . . . look to those who have been excluded and placed on the margins . . . It is that the place for creative hope that arises out of suffering is most likely now to be found among blacks, women, and homosexuals. These outcasts may well be the custodians of those thin places . . . watchers at the frontiers between what is and what is to be."[2]

I recall sharing communion in a dirt-floored, corrugated metal shack with peasants in El Salvador, sitting amidst scratching chickens and squalling babies with military gun ship helicopters roaring overheard looking to squash the very rebels we were with. And yet those rebels, most of whom had lost family members in their battle for justice, were joyful as we shared communion.

"Like yeast that a woman took and mixed in . . . " Bent fingers. Thin place.

I think of sitting where small candles cast large shadows on the bare walls of a room in Cape Haitian, Haiti. For hours our delegation listened to stories of brutality told by people on the run, hunted by the military dictators of that desperately poor country. The next morning we went with a young priest to take communion in a shabby chapel with people dressed in rags but radiance in their faces and lives.

"Mustard seed . . . becomes a tree so that the birds . . . make nests in its branches." Bent fingers. Thin place.

I think of talking to black South Africans before dawn as they stood in line to vote in the country's first all-race election. Many were barefoot, women carrying babies in slings on their backs, men leaning on crutches, kids clutching parents' legs, old people carried by friends for miles but all serene in their commitment to merciful justice. I think of worshiping in an evangelical church in South Africa one Sunday at which the pastor urged his poor, black congregation not to be bitter or vengeful.

"A man took a seed and sowed it . . ." Bent fingers. Thin place.

When life is stripped down to its essence, when people who have so little of the material things we take for granted, yet show a spirit of compassion, of hope, of faith, of community that our society seems to have lost, I understand a little of what inclusion is and comfort is. It is we who are being included by those people in what life comes down to. It comes down to the thin places, and we dare not miss them.

We are gifts to each other, the poor to us as much as we to them. Roberta Bondi teaches prayer, and I keep going back to something she said: "Our human relations are mirrors of our relationship with God." That is a clear, hard truth, but potentially a comforting one.

God touches us with comfort when we touch each other with honesty and compassion. That's what it means to be custodians of the thin places. That is what justice and trust in our family life is about, and what justice and reconciliation in our social and political life is about, at the core. That is what life together in the church is about, or should be, as well as our mission as a church is about. That is what each of us is about as we pray, sing, reach out, touch, include, let ourselves be included, risk giving the gift God made us.

A young person once said to the great violinist Fritz Kreisler, "I'd give my life to play as beautifully as you do." Kreisler replied, "I did." Well . . .

"The kingdom of heaven is like a mustard seed that a man took and sowed . . . like yeast that a woman took and mixed in . . ."

So we come to the other side of the parables and of the thin places—God's side. It is by far the most crucial side. Think of it this way. Both the man and the woman in the parables "took" something given and did something with it: the man with the seed, the woman with the yeast. God gave it and God was in it. They simply took what was given, lived it, and something like miracles happened.

Faith, or better yet, trust, is the bridge at the thin place. That's why these two parables of Jesus are parables of trust, of faith, and so of comfort and hope. The trust is that God is at work in our lives, invisibly at work, like a seed growing in the darkness, like yeast rising in the loaf. The work of faith is to identify and make sense of the thin places. That means never losing heart. It means to keep taking, and planting, and mixing in faith. It is no accident that small acts affect lives far beyond our view, our power, our lifetime. That's true because God is faithful. God is at work in the invisible world that rubs against, and breaks through, into this visible one, while remaining invisible to us. The haunt of grace is like light that makes itself known by what it touches. God's presence is invisible, but invincible at last.

Recently I read a review of a book by physicist Robert Osserman entitled *Poetry of the Universe*—a wonderful title —with the subtitle *Mathematical Exploration of the Cosmos*. The book is about mapping the universe, and I didn't understand much except the reviewer's final words: "The reader of this little book will know why cosmologists use words like 'beauty,' 'music' and 'poetry' to describe the mysterious nature of our universe." I find that comforting. It frees us from the stifling idea that science will one day explain all the mysteries away and run God out of the neighborhood. Beauty, music, poetry go deeper than explanations. So does God!

For fun, and instruction, here is one more quote from a science writer named Cramer: "If you stand in the dark and look at a star a hundred light-years away and think that what it's telling you is that a hundred years in the past, the advance waves that are returning to the star from your eyes shook hands with the electrons in the star, encouraging it to send light in your direction—well it makes you feel sort of shivery." Yes, it does, even if you don't get it, and a better word for shivery is awe.

The point is this: The God who created all this, and is creating it still, is bigger, more ingenious, sneakier than we can pin down with our creeds and theories. A book on the great Indian leader Crazy Horse helps focus what that suggests spiritually. Once, when Crazy Horse was enraged about what was happening to his people, he went outside the lodge tent into the night where "the sky was far and there was room for an angry man."

What I am trying to say is that God—the kingdom of the invisible world rubbing against this one—has room enough for angry people, people who grieve and cry, frightened people, people who doubt and betray, are guilty of all sorts of sin, who struggle, get sick and die, yet do wonderful, beautiful, incredible things. People like us. God holds us, like the earth holds a seed, breaks us open, raises us like life from a seed, like yeast raises the mess of flour and makes bread of it, of us. That is what God's grace, God's mercy, God's power and purposes are about. At the thin places we are—at the thin places we seek and find and share—God is there, invisibly, invincibly working. The bent fingers are a clue.

And so is this story I heard at the Orthodox Jewish wedding

of Jason and Meredith last summer. At the wedding reception, Meredith's father, a professor at Princeton, gave her and Jason a pair of silver candlesticks and explained where they'd come from. During World War II in Amsterdam, Nazis knocked on the doors of Jews and demanded all their silver. One family was a friend of a man named Walter Kauffman, a colleague of Meredith's father. Well, the family gave all their silver except four candlesticks. Then the family was sent to a concentration camp where all died except the father, the friend of Professor Kauffman.

After the war, the man returned to his home but it was burned down and nothing remained but charred rubble. While he was standing there crying in the rubble, a neighbor came and said that they'd thought everything was lost in the fire. But one day, as they poked through the rubble, they came upon the four candlesticks, burned, twisted but not destroyed. They had saved them for the family in case any of them ever came back after the war. They gave the candlesticks to that father as they all stood there in the ruins.

Later, the father gave the candlesticks to his friend, Walter Kauffman. When Walter came to the United States, he gave the candlesticks to Meredith's father. After telling the story, her father gave the candlesticks to Meredith and Jason on their wedding day. The gift was given as we gathered in a synagogue, all of which the Nazis set out to blot from the face of the earth. I watched and listened with tears in my eyes but a smile on my face. Twisted silver candlesticks carrying the light of God's covenant with the Jewish people, and all of us, which the darkness of the Holocaust could not snuff out. Death could not, did not, cannot defeat God or the life God gives us.

A terminally ill young mother telling a beautiful story through her tears and smile; two tiny hands with bent fingers. Two young people, a wedding, and twisted candlesticks. A man who took . . . yea, thousands of men who take mustard seeds and plant them. A woman who took . . . yea, thousands of women who take yeast and mix it. Each of us. All of us. Herein, and all around, is comfort and hope.

∼

1.   Peter J. Gomes, *The Good Book: Reading the Bible with Mind and Heart* (New York: William Morrow and Company, Inc., 1996), 214.

2.   Ibid., 230.

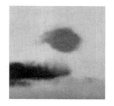

How Far Is One?

Psalm 130
Mark 10:2-16

I put off publicly addressing this issue as long as I could—perhaps even longer. I put it off because it's painful. I put it off because I did not want to use a public forum to try to justify myself, or anyone else, by distorting or misrepresenting things, which is an easy and human thing to do. I put it off because I am a divorced and remarried man. And yet, I'm ordained and committed to wrestle with what Jesus says about hard, painful things such as divorce and remarriage. I can no longer avoid doing so with any integrity.

Probably you're familiar with what he said on the subject. But just so I won't be the only one squirming, let me repeat it. Cut to the chase. Jesus agrees with the Pharisees who question him that divorce is permissible by the law of Moses. Then he goes on, "But from the beginning of creation, 'God made them male and female.' For this reason, a man shall . . . be joined to his wife, and the two shall become one flesh . . . Therefore what God has joined together, let no one separate . . . Whoever divorces his wife and marries another commits adultery against her; and if she divorces her husband and marries another, she commits adultery."

There it is, stark and unsettling. I put off addressing it until, at last, it dawned on me that what Jesus is saying is really the gospel in miniature. That is, it's "good news" at heart—bad at first, hard always, but good all the way in. To tell you why it is, let me share a few simple, ungarnished truths that have come from my struggle with what Jesus says, as well as from my own experience.

The truth I want to share could be summed up by saying there is really no such thing as divorce. Not really! Legally, yes, but not psychologically, or morally, or spiritually. It seems to me that this is what Jesus is saying, and my experience confirms it. Divorce isn't just a legal matter. It isn't even primarily a moral issue, though there are moral issues involved. It isn't primarily a moral issue because it really isn't about what we should do, or should not do.

Before anything else, it's about what we *cannot* do. Jesus says we cannot actually terminate our relationships with each other because God made us for each other, and nothing can ever change that. We can abuse, hurt, betray, oppress, exploit, even leave each other, but finally we cannot break our connections to each other. Those connections are braided into creation itself and into our core. They are grounded in God. The inescapable truth is that whatever any one of us does affects all of us, one way or another. It continues to do so, especially in marriage, or after it.

It's a terrible, destructive illusion to think we are ever done with each other. Death does not end a relationship between people, it just changes the way the relationship works. That's how it is with divorce. Divorce does not end the relationship between people, it just changes it. When two become one flesh, as Jesus put it, it isn't just about sharing sex, it's about sharing selves. Sharing selves as openly and deeply as two people can. That experience becomes part of each self. So the relationship continues to affect both parties even after they think they are divorced. My divorce continues to affect me and always will. A divorce continues to affect all persons involved, especially the children but also the entire family,

friends, institutions—*even as does a marriage*. It is important to see
that. Even as marriage is not the solution for most problems neither is divorce the solution for most problems. Even as marriage
is not the cause of most problems, neither is divorce. I know
that's how it works for me and for Dory, my first wife.

Morality has to do with the way we relate to each other. But
that we *have* to relate to each other, for good or ill, is rooted in
God's purposes for us. God intends for us to live together, to
love, to be just and fair, to treat each other as equals, to be accountable for what we do, whether we fulfill those purposes or
not. And we never fulfill them completely.

Of course, we can help and bless each other, and we do. But
we can also betray and hurt each other, and we do. It is never just
one or the other in any relationship. Still, there are always consequences to our betrayals: When we betray others, we also betray
and hurt ourselves. It's unavoidable and it's true in the relationships not only of husbands and wives but of parents and children,
of siblings, of partners in any relationship.

It's also true of relationships between black, white, His-
panic, Asian, rich, poor, middle-class people, gay and straight
people, whomever. Legally, politically, economically, geograph-
ically we can separate, but in our core, our souls, our very being,
we cannot. In the deepest sense, there is no such thing as divorce.

"What God has joined together, let no one separate."

What's the point of insisting there's really no such thing as
divorce? For one thing, it means that we cannot dehumanize, demean, and discard someone as though that would solve anything
or make us better. It means we can't truly blame others for our
problems. I am sick of the blame game we all play. I am sick that
the blame game is epidemic in our society. "Nothing is ever my
responsibility. If something is wrong it's because of what someone else did." Nonsense! The truth is that one marriage partner
cannot say, "If only my spouse would shape up, things would be

fine." Nor can one partner say, "If only I could find someone who would understand and appreciate me, my life would be great." Those statements are simply untrue.

The honest truth is that we bless each other, and we give good gifts to each other over the years in marriage and in all relationships. There is some healing in a relationship when that is recognized and affirmed. It helped me, and to some extent it helped our broken relationship when, after a time, I could express gratitude to Dory for her many gifts to me and to our children, gifts which continue to bless us.

Many years ago, when people came to me to perform their weddings, I would set up several premarital counseling sessions. Then I noticed that the couple's eyes kept glazing over. Since then I've gotten premarital counseling down to six words: "When you need help, get it." What I mean is that in times of romance, we think relationships are easy and natural, no sweat, a piece of cake. That is not so! Human relationships are the most difficult yet most basic, essential, and rewarding element of life. So they take work. Love involves work!

No matter who we are, we cannot be everything or mean everything to another person, or to anything else. When we have medical issues, we know the consequences of ignoring them. So we go to a doctor. Yet when we have relational issues, we think we can handle them by ourselves. Probably we can't! The same is true of relational issues as of medical or legal issues.

So when—not if, *when*—we have relational issues, we need to be ready and mutually agreeable to make the effort to get help. Just as we get tune-ups for our cars, we sometimes need to get tune-ups for our marriages. Go to someone who can help, a family therapist or someone you trust who can help each of you face yourself. Go before problems fester. There's no stigma in getting help, but there can be a stunting of the relationship if we don't. And get help if you are considering divorce and thinking that if you can get away from the other person, all will be well.

"When you need help, get it."

God gives us many options. Prayer and spiritual nurture together can be a help. The community of faith can be a resource if the people in it are honest and willing to share with each other at that deeper level and not be content with some feel-good, avoid-hard-things superficiality. My deep hope for the church is that it be that kind of healing, redeeming body of grace.

But for grace to become real for us, we need to claim it. Trusting grace in moments not only of gladness but of conflict, and opening ourselves to it even in tough circumstances, is what deepens and stretches our love for each other. That's part of what I mean by the hard work of love.

God's grace comes to us through many people, including therapists. I know that from my own experience. I went to therapy before my divorce. I went during and after my divorce. We did family therapy sessions that were painful and helpful. I had to face myself so I would not just repeat with someone else what happened with Dory. I had to face the injury I had done to Dory, and to my children. I had to hear the hard truth my children spoke to me about my failures, my temper, my lack of understanding, my authoritarian demands, my not being around for them enough. They listened to my side as well.

There were tears and anger and guilt and healing in it. Out of it came a different kind of relationship between my kids and me that's closer, more honest and trusting than it ever was or ever would have been without that hard, ongoing, even redemptive, work. Divorce, like marriage, can tilt toward mercy, growth, and grace.

The wonder is that a crisis in a relationship blows it open and makes something different possible for everyone, if we work at it. It is in the mess of human life that moral action takes place, or not. Morality is rooted in the awareness that God makes connection the essential condition of our humanity, and it cannot be ignored or denied without shrinking love to a fleeting feeling. Fairness, justice, and love are inseparable.

So Jan, my wife now, and I revel in our relationship yet keep plugging away at it at the same time. The plugging away never ends, thank God. Literally, thank God because it means we take our love, and God's, seriously. There are no perfect marriages, no perfect relationships, no perfect parents, no perfect people because none of us is God, even if we think we are. The hard truth is we continue to disappoint and hurt each other, and yet at the same time we fulfill and give each other joy. Relationships are complicated, confusing sometimes. But we can tilt our relationships more toward the fulfillment side.

Love isn't just about feelings. It's about building trust, because finally there is no love without trust. Love involves work. That's spelled out all through the Bible. Look how hard Moses and the prophets worked. Look how hard Jesus worked, and the disciples and Peter. What else but love works that hard, that deeply, that long? But, oh, how it is worth it. I am profoundly blessed by the work of love Jan presses us to do together, even in those times I'm tempted to shirk it.

Am I committing adultery with her because she and I are both divorced and re-married? I don't really believe so. If I am, God have mercy on me. But surely I would be unfaithful if I avoided the emotional and spiritual intimacy of telling her my side, my truth, and hearing her side, her truth, meeting and engaging each other, and trying to negotiate fairly with each other. That's how trust is built, and without trust what happens to love?

I would be unfaithful if I didn't work at building trust with her. That is what intimacy is about, not just sex. You see, betrayal can be cold-blooded, not just hot-blooded. We betray each other when we lie, distort, manipulate out of a hidden agenda. We betray each other when we avoid the hard stuff, when we treat each other as things to be used for our own gratification or glorification. We betray each other when we retreat into silence and become inaccessible. And to betray others is to betray ourselves and God because there's no such thing as divorce.

Surely, it doesn't take rocket science or artistic genius to connect the dots from intimate to more inclusive relations. We can stretch what Jesus says about marriage and divorce to our relationships with all kinds of other people. We can be more inclusive in our connections with people of another color or race or nationality or creed or gender or sexual orientation because those connections cannot be broken without terrible, destructive consequences. If we haven't learned that yet, it's time we did.

I strongly believe our sexual orientations are mysteriously given to us in the same way our gender or race is. So I also believe that relationships between homosexual persons should be recognized as being as legally and spiritually valid as are those of heterosexual persons. That is only just and fair. It means we all play on the same, level field and are accountable to the same standards for our behavior. When Jesus spoke about creating us male and female, so that what God joins together no one should separate, I do not believe he was excluding homosexuals from the sacredness of partnership covenants. The same truth applies to all human relationships, heterosexual and homosexual, racial, gender, nationality, whatever. What God has joined together, let no one separate!

To see and celebrate our inviolable human connections is what the foundation of justice is about. Without a spiritual depth to it, social action atrophies and dies. That's why Jesus spent so much of his time among those his society had pushed to the margins. But—and this is important, too—he also spent time with the enemies of those marginalized people, and his own enemies. He met them constantly, went to Jerusalem to confront them. Jesus demonstrated that to love our enemies does not mean to be afraid to make them. To love them means not to dismiss or demonize them. As in a marriage, so in social action: We need to be done blaming other persons and groups for what is wrong. We need to begin dealing straight up with them, advocating, arguing, but still treating them as human beings. We need to get on as best we can in simply doing the work of justice where we are, and to do it with some degree of humility as well as passion.

Morality and justice are rooted in the religious awareness of our connectedness not just with people we like and agree with, but with people we don't like or agree with. It is a spiritual issue, not just political or ideological. There is really no such thing as divorce, and it is a dangerous and destructive illusion to think or act otherwise.

I said at the outset that finally it came to me that what Jesus says about divorce and remarriage is good news—not good advice, but good news—however hard or bad it seems at first. How is it good news? How is it the gospel in miniature? Because the gospel, the good news, isn't primarily about morality, it's about grace. The good news is there is no such thing as divorce from God, either. Not really. And here is how I see that.

Go back to the family therapy room with me, and to meetings in our various family living rooms, and to long tearful nights of praying and pacing. You see, what I heard from my children, and from Dory, wasn't so much about the injury I inflicted through the divorce, though there certainly was that. It was about the injuries I inflicted all through the marriage, long before the divorce. I didn't intend those injuries. Mostly, we never do. I did the best I could, and so do most of us, most of the time.

But the best I do, the best any of us do, is seldom if ever grounds for much pride or self-congratulation. Oh, yes, we have wondrous gifts and skills, do good things, are amazingly creative, contribute to others in critical ways, are valuable persons. And yet, we still inflict serious injuries on each other and ourselves. We are limited, mortal beings. We are finite in power, incomplete in knowledge, ambivalent in motives, restricted in determining outcomes of actions. We consistently fall short of the kind of personal integrity or marital fulfillment Jesus pointed to when he spoke of marriage as "two becoming one flesh."

But I wonder, in faith, if by using term "flesh" Jesus wasn't confirming all our limitations as well as our possibilities. I wonder if he wasn't saying that marriage is about sharing our limitations as well as our strengths, so that we are each made more whole through that continual process of honest, hard sharing. Maybe what he meant by "one" wasn't a kind of fusion of two persons into one, but rather two persons entering into one process of sharing, of challenging, confronting, forgiving, enjoying, growing as two persons coming together in one process. It's intriguing to imagine it that way, isn't it? And more compatible with the way Jesus went about living.

If there is some truth in that view, then marriage isn't so much two people looking in each others eyes as it is two people side by side looking at the horizon toward which they are moving together. Both the moving and the horizon are the essence of marriage. I believe that is true of all human relationships, from the intimate to the global.

So we come to the question that's the title of this reflection: "How Far Is One?" Part of the truth is that it's as far as the horizon. We never get there in this lifetime. It's beyond our reach, our power. We fail, as I failed in my first marriage, as both of us did. We all fail in our relationships, our best efforts, our lives. Oh, not completely, for to say that would be false modesty, and false modesty is at least half pride.

And yet, there's a Russian proverb that says, "To walk toward spring is to become the spring." It's a compelling image, and we grasp what it means. Then it is also compelling, and true, that *to walk toward the horizon is to become the horizon.*

Now we ask the question again: "How Far is One?" Yes, it is as far as the horizon. And yet it is as near as the next step we take toward it. So trust steps out on that promise. It moves, step by step, and we become, at least a little, the justice and beauty and forgiveness and joy we long for off there on the horizon.

Most deeply, it is God's grace we long for, some wholeness beyond our limitations and faults and failures. How far is such wholeness, such oneness with God? As far as the horizon. But the mystery is that it is by God's grace that we move and live and have our being. It is by God's grace that we walk step by step toward the wholeness for which we long. It is by God's grace that we walk together, when we risk it. And with each step, we become a little more of the oneness, that wholeness. Because grace is also as close as those steps. I hang on to that, or it hangs on to me, every step of every day, or I'd be lost.

What, then, of divorce, mine or anyone's? What of human brokenness in all it's terrifying variations? Come with me to the soul-trembling closing scene of Leonard Bernstein's *Mass*. I have heard it many times on my CD, but I've never seen it except in my imagination. Well, actually I've seen a picture of the scene in the little brochure of the lyrics that comes with the CD. In that scene a priest carrying a glass chalice and wearing beautiful vestments climbs up a staircase where he is to celebrate the Mass. For a moment he towers over the people. He begins the prayers and the choir sings. Then, at the moment he elevates the glass chalice, he hurls it to the floor as if in protest of the distance he and the Mass are from the people. Then he descends from his high station, removes his vestments and kneels among the shards of the shattered chalice. He begins to sing these words:

> Look . . . Isn't that—odd.
> Glass shines—brighter—
> When it's broken . . .
> I never noticed that.[1]

There's the haunt of grace, the mystery of the crucifixion and resurrection.

Broken chalice, broken marriage, broken relationships, broken dreams, broken hearts, broken lives. Yet, sometimes, many times, maybe most times, they shine brighter when they're broken because the light that shines to make them brighter is one no darkness can overcome. So we, in our brokenness walk together toward that light, that horizon, and become more whole. It's not far and yet it takes forever. Walk in peace.

∼

1.   Leonard Bernstein, *Mass: A Theater Piece for Singers, Players and Dancers*, Sony Classical SM2K 63089.

X's and O's

The Song of Solomon

The Song of Solomon is so romantic and so explicitly erotic that there were those who argued to ban it from the Bible back when the canon was originally approved. There are those who would ban it today. *The Song of Solomon* was finally included in the biblical canon because others argued that it is a love song to God and from God. In any case, it is in Scripture, a wonderful, graphic, poetic, vivid love song. I recommend that you find someone you love and read it aloud to each other.

HUGS AND KISSES*

Let him kiss me with the kisses of his mouth!
For your love is better than wine,
your anointing oils are fragrant,
your name is perfume poured out;
therefore the maidens love you.
Draw me after you, let us make haste.
The king has brought me into his chambers.
We will exult and rejoice in you;
we will extol your love more than wine;
rightly do they love you.
—The Song of Solomon 1:2-4

* When this reflection was originally presented as a sermon, musical interludes were offered between each section.

I suppose my earliest self-conscious expression of love was in thank-you letters to aunts and uncles and grandparents for presents they sent. At the end of the tortured, downhill-tilted lines, just after my name, I added several X's and O's to represent hugs and kisses. Every kid did that. So every kid learned that the trick was to add as many X's and O's as would fill up the page so the actual letter could be short. The X's and O's were the real message anyway. The only thing was that I wanted to give the relatives I loved best more X's and O's than the others, but probably no one noticed the difference anyway. Besides, I was always confused about whether the X's were the kisses and the O's the hugs, or vice versa. But the hugs and kisses *were* the real message.

We are constantly receiving mixed messages about what "true love" is. Out of the many conflicting cultural icons of love, Valentine's Day is one of the most familiar. Yet Valentine was actually a priest in the eleventh century who became the patron saint of romantic love. His message was that all love is pure and holy, not just some love.

If we read the first lines from *The Song of Solomon* carefully, the message of Valentine, and of hugs and kisses, comes through: Down with all the barriers we've put up to differentiate between romantic love and spiritual love, or between the love of friends and the love of sexual partners. Down with the barriers between the love of justice and the love of beauty, or the love of humans and the love of nature, and all the other distinctions we make between platonic and erotic and spiritual love.

Of course there are differences, but the message is they are all of a piece, all rooted in the grace of God. They are all hints of the Lover who created us and everything else, and who loves us and the whole creation.

When we get that message, there are freedom and delight, awe and joy in it. It opens us to God in different and new ways, on every hand and every area of life. The message is that when we love anything or anyone, we're close to God. Or, better, God is close to us.

CATCHING THE LITTLE FOXES

The voice of my beloved!
Look, he comes, leaping upon the mountains,
bounding over the hills.
My beloved is like a gazelle or a young stag.
Look, there he stands behind our wall,
gazing in at the windows,
looking through the lattice.
My beloved speaks and says to me:
"Arise, my love, my fair one, and come away;
for now, the winter is past,
the rain is over and gone.
The flowers appear on the earth,
the time of singing has come,
and the voice of the turtledove is heard in our land.
The fig tree puts forth its figs,
and the vines are in blossom;
they give forth fragrance.
Arise, my love, my fair one, and come away.
O my dove, in the clefts of the rock,
in the covert of the cliff,
let me see your face,
let me hear your voice;
for your voice is sweet, and your face is lovely.
Catch us the foxes, the little foxes,
that ruin the vineyards—
for our vineyards are in blossom.
—The Song of Solomon 2:8-15

"*The time of singing has come,*" says the lover ecstatically in *The Song of Solomon*, and we know what he means. Lovers sing. They can't help it. But then the lover's song modulates to a whispered warning to all lovers: "*Catch us the foxes, the little foxes, that ruin the vineyards—for our vineyards are in blossom.*"

What does that mean? It means that love is not just song, it is work. Little foxes are always eating away at the blossoms of it. So go to work for love; catch the little foxes, the singer implores. Stop them before they ruin love's vineyards.

Little foxes. What are they? Well, the funny thing about love is how awkward and embarrassed it can make us. Why so? Because to love we have to give up control, and that makes us feel foolish. But if we aren't willing to be a seen as at least a little foolish, we're a stranger to love. And that's the dilemma of it.

Something Amos Oz wrote hints at it. He describes being a boy living in Jerusalem in 1943. It was a time when life was hanging by a thread for the Jews, and for the world. So Amos' family wrote a letter to Uncle Zvi and his wife, who lived in Tel Aviv. The letter set an exact time for a long-distance telephone call to them: Wednesday, the nineteenth at five o'clock.

In a few days, a confirming letter came back. Since neither family had a telephone in their house, the call was to be made from the Oz family neighborhood pharmacy in Jerusalem to Uncle Zvi's neighborhood pharmacy in Tel Aviv. So a major event was put in place with all the support strategies. All week before the phone call, Amos's family reminded each other of the impending call, warning each other not to schedule or get involved in anything that would interfere with the plans for Wednesday, the nineteenth at five o'clock. Everyone had to pledge not to be late coming home from work or school that day.

On Wednesday the nineteenth, the entire family put on their best clothes and went to the pharmacy to make the call. In-

variably they arrived early and sat nervously waiting, not wanting to make the call until the exact minute so they would be sure
the family in Tel Aviv would be there. When the moment came,
Amos's father, Aryeh, made the call.

Finally, the connection was made, and the conversation
went like this:

"Hello, Zvi."

"Speaking."

"This is Aryeh calling from Jerusalem."

"Hello, Aryeh. This is Zvi. How are you all? Everything is
fine at this end. We are talking to you from the pharmacy."

"Same here. What's new?"

"Nothing special."

"How are things going, Zvi?"

"There's nothing new in particular. How are things with
you?"

"Fine. No news here."

"Well, no news is good news."

"Yes, indeed, everything is excellent. And now Fania wants
to speak to you."

Fania was Amos's mother. She got on the phone, and it was
the same thing all over again. "How are you?" . . . "Fine." . . .
"What's new?" . . . "Nothing. You?" . . . "Everything is fine,"
and so on and on. It ended with the promise to write and the setting of a time for the next call, and then the goodbyes: "We'll
talk again soon." . . . "Yes. It's good to hear your voice." . . .
"Take care." . . . "All the best to you."

Later, an adult Oz reflected on those 1943-44 boyhood
telephone conversations: "Now I know this was not at all
funny. Life was hanging by a thread . . . they were not at all
sure they would ever speak again. God knows what was
about to happen . . . I realize how hard it was for them to
express personal feelings. Public sentiment was no prob-

lem. They were highly emotional people. They could passionately argue about Bakunin or about Trotsky. They could reach the verge of tears debating colonialism, or exploitation or anti-Semitism, but when they wanted to convey a personal emotion, they were struck dumb . . . arid, clenched, even terrified, the heritage of many generations of suppression . . . Almost everything was considered improper."[1]

Recognize any of the symptoms? Even so, *"Catch us . . . the little foxes, that ruin the vineyards."* What little foxes? Well, how is it we're so good at analyzing, criticizing, planning, suggesting, advising, correcting, complaining, arguing, surfing the internet in our heads, and yet so shy about saying what is in our hearts, about thanking, complimenting, confirming, telling someone we love him or her? How is it we're so good at running institutions, running neighborhoods, running projects, even running the world . . . and so good as well at running from intimacy, honest sharing, being close?

Maybe it helps to keep remembering that life is always hanging in the balance, and the next time to speak, to show love, may never come. Maybe it helps to remember that we have to be a little foolish, a little childlike and vulnerable to make those X's and O's real, to answer the call of the Lover in our hearts to *"Arise . . . and come away."* To come away from the clench and the stifling habits and let someone see our real face. To hear our truest voice, to touch our deepest heart. To catch the little foxes that ruin our vineyards before it is too late.

KISSING THE BEAST

Upon my bed at night
I sought him whom my soul loves;
I sought him, but found him not;
I called him, but he gave no answer.
"I will rise now and go about the city,
in the streets and in the squares;
I will seek him whom my soul loves."
I sought him, but found him not.
The sentinels found me,
as they went about in the city.
"Have you seen him whom my soul loves?"
Scarcely had I passed them,
when I found him whom my soul loves.
I held him, and would not let him go
until I brought him into my mother's house,
and into the chamber of her that conceived me.
I adjure you, O daughters of Jerusalem,
by the gazelles or the wild does:
do not stir up nor awaken love until it is ready.
—The Song of Solomon 3:1-5

In this portion of *The Song of Solomon*, when the beloved can't find the lover, she goes to look for him. Where does she look? She looks in the streets and squares of the city. Without being too literal about it, there's an X and O message in that.

I've always been a sucker for the story of *Beauty and the Beast*. Everyone knows the story: The beautiful Princess meets the frightening, ugly, deformed beast but instead of running away, as everyone else does, she stays with him. Finally she kisses him, and at that moment the beast becomes a handsome man.

The thing is, it's more than a fairy tale. It touches a primal truth. I've been kissed like that, though looking at me you might not know it. But this beast has been kissed like that, a thousand times, and each one has changed my heart. It happens. You may know that from your own experience.

So here's the point: Love is about personal relationships. But not all those personal relationships are private. Not all of them should be. Love relationships are public, too, and they have public consequences. These days, the city is seen as frightening and ugly by lots of people who run from it. But the city is nothing but a complex network of people. Society is people. Welfare is about people. Poverty is about people. Racial justice is about people. Health care, schools, crime, violence, drugs are all about people. The beast of the city, of society, of the nation, the world, awaits our kiss.

But as long as we *talk* about issues and statistics, we can run and hide. As long as we talk in the abstract about financial markets, about taxes, about Social Security and Medicare, we can take cover in bloodless, heady, impersonal debate. Yet issues change when they take on a human face.

Justice is love on the prowl, like the beloved in *The Song of Solomon* looking for her lover in the city streets, the night streets that are scary, the city streets where people, human beings, pursue their dreams or sweep up the broken pieces of them. Justice is love on the prowl, trying to kiss the beast, trying to put a human face on the issues of poverty and sickness and homelessness and welfare families and all the rest.

Yes, of course, politics are involved, and economics, and finances and tough choices. But first of all, it's about love. Love on the prowl. Lovers like us go on the prowl looking for the people, putting a face on things, trying to kiss the fear away outside and inside, and so finding their hearts and our own. For the simple truth is that the Lover we are all looking for is God, and the face under all faces is that of Christ. This means we are each and every one beasts turned beloved by the kiss of God. We are the ones who have been kissed a thousand times. Think about that and sing.

Then move out! For we are the ones sent on the prowl to find and to kiss the beast of our time in our cities, our society, our nation and planet. To kiss that beast, if not to make it handsome, more importantly to find and set free its heart—and in the mystery of love to find and free our own.

SEAL ON THE HEART

Set me as a seal upon your heart,
as a seal upon your arm;
for love is strong as death,
passion fierce as the grave.
Its flashes are flashes of fire,
a raging flame.
Many waters cannot quench love,
neither can floods drown it.
If one offered for love
all the wealth of one's house,
it would be utterly scorned.
—*The Song of Solomon* 8:6-7

I get a catch in my throat whenever I read this passage from *The Song of Solomon.* The Lover says, *"Set me as a seal upon your heart."* Isn't that what God is forever saying to us? Isn't that what God is forever doing for us and with us? Isn't that what the cross and the empty tomb are about? Isn't that what the fumbling company of the church across the centuries, and today, is or ought to be about? Isn't that what the moments of love we have all known are about, all those touches and glimpses of it that tiptoe into our hearts like stars into the darkness, like a lover stretching out on the shore of body and soul as the sea stretches out on the sand? All love is of a piece, all our loves hint of the Eternal Lover.

John Polkinghorne is an Anglican Priest and a world-class physicist who made this accurate statement: "Transparent moments of encounter with the sacred can neither be induced nor repeated through human contrivance, but only received."[2] Only received. And yet, we so much want such transparent moments of encounter with the sacred, such a relationship with the Eternal Lover, that we try desperately to earn them, to work to get them as a reward, to prove we are worthy of them. Often in those efforts, good things happen. But the truth is that moments of encounter with the sacred can only be received.

The Song of Solomon puts it graphically: *"If one offered for love all the wealth of one's house, it would be utterly scorned."* All the wealth of our house, our good works, our smarts and successes, our poetry and prophetic clamoring, whatever else they are about, love is not it. At least, it's not about God's love. God's love is received, not achieved.

But the good news is that God's love is already ours. God's seal is already set upon our hearts. Receiving it is just a matter of being foolish enough to brush the dust off our hearts and saying back to God, "I love you, too." Many waters cannot quench love. Not God's love. Not our love. Not really.

X's and O's to us all.

~

1. Story and quote from "Chekhov In Hebrew," Amos Oz, *The New Yorker*, December 25, 1995, and January 1, 1996: 50-65.

2. John Polkinghorne at a conference on "Science and the Spiritual Quest," Berkeley, CA, 1991.

Mind What's Left

John 5:1-9

Alice and Violet are talking. They are two black women in Toni Morrison's powerful novel *Jazz*. Both women are in their fifties. They've not been friends even though they live in the same apartment building in Harlem. But their pain has brought them together.

Violet is the wife of Joe. Joe had become the lover of Alice's eighteen-year-old niece, an orphan Alice had raised from childhood. Joe is suspected of having killed the young woman when she broke off the affair, but there's no way to prove it.

Now Violet, cramped with anguish, slashes out at Alice's niece for causing it by seducing her husband. Alice listens as she continues with her ironing. Violet rakes Joe over the coals of her lament. She threatens to throw him out. Then she pleads with Alice, "We women, me and you. Tell me something real. Don't just say I'm grown and ought to know. I don't . . . What about it? Do I stay with him? . . ."

The two women talk on for a time. Finally, out of the depths of her own suffering, Alice says to Violet, "You want a real thing? I'll tell you a real one. You got anything left to you to love, anything at all, do it."

Violet is taken aback. "And when he does it again? Don't mind what people think?"

"Mind what's left to you," Alice answers.

"You saying take it? Don't fight?"

"Fight what, who? . . . Nobody's asking you to take it. I'm sayin make it, make it!"

Suddenly they become aware of the smoke rising from where Alice had put down her iron. Alice swears.

> Violet was the first to smile. Then Alice. In no time laughter was rocking them both . . . and suddenly the world was right side up. Violet learned then what she had forgotten until this moment: that laughter is serious. More complicated, more serious than tears.[1]

Such a wonderful scene, and we're in it. Just as are Violet and Alice, everyone is injured in some way. Everyone has a pocket full of losses, harbors some kind of painful wound, walks with some sort of limp. So, as did Violet, all of us know the subtle temptation to consider ourselves victims. It's easy to slip into that mode, and most of us are good at it. We can play the victim at the drop of an inconvenience.

But to do that trivializes the mystery of God's grace and providence. There are two loose ways to trivialize or domesticate God. One is to claim to know what God should and will do without question, as those of us who are conservatives or fundamentalists do. The other is to claim to know what God can't and won't do, as those of us who are progressives and intellectuals do. Faith walks the tightrope between the two domestications. Faith lives in that tension. That is the risk and creativity of it.

One of the reasons I get uneasy in many social gatherings is because there's frequently an undercurrent of a martyr syndrome, a "poor us, we ought to sue them" mentality to much of the conversation. There seem to be endless variations of that lament. Often I'm ready to sing my own version of it. But more often I'm reminded of Flannery O'Connor being asked by a frustrated author if university teachers stifled writers. She answered, "My opinion is they don't stifle enough of them. There's many a best seller that could have been prevented by a good teacher."

Ditto whatever "Poor Us Inc." we're a member of. Ditto victims of all stripes and subtleties who might be prevented by a good teacher, an honest friend, a thoughtful self-examination, and a hard work-out with the mystery of God.

Of course, everyone's wounds are real. Everyone's struggle is hard. Affliction isn't irrelevant. But those truths aren't the real point. The real point is, *"You got anything left to you to love, anything at all, do it . . . Mind what's left to you."* The haunt of grace is that there's always something left to us, and in us, to love.

Which means that celebration, like laughter, is serious, complicated business. In *A River Runs Through It*, a beautiful book from which a movie of the same title was made, Norman says of his Presbyterian minister father, who taught him fly fishing and religion, "To him, all good things—trout as well as eternal salvation—come by grace and grace comes by art, and art does not come easy."[2]

In Scripture there is a story about Jesus by the Bethesda pool in Jerusalem. The tradition was that whenever the water of the pool churned up, it was because a passing angel had disturbed it. Then the first one into the roiling water got healed. Obviously, there were lots of invalids hanging around waiting for the water to roil. (I'll pass on the temptation to suggest the ways you and I might wait around for our version of water to roil.)

One man had been by the pool for thirty-eight years. Thirty-eight years! He's a career victim, a Ph.D. passive-aggressive. He's probably a nice guy but with a secret rage about what God couldn't and wouldn't do for him. There's no mystery for him, and no celebration. Just a life settled into a rut with no "real thing" to shake and sustain him.

Can't you imagine him camped out by the pool, using his affliction (whatever it was, since the story doesn't say) to con people into feeling sorry for him and running his errands? Can't you hear him complaining in well-modulated, seductive tones about how unfair his fate is? It's a familiar gig. We've all played a few notes of it. It isn't so much that the man is an invalid as it is that he's *in-valid*, a bit of a fraud.

Jesus doesn't chat him up, or hold his hand, or take a history. He just does two things that demonstrate the art of grace and the heart of celebration. One thing is down and dirty. The other, quick and clean.

First, Jesus asks the man, "Do you want to be made well?" That's down and dirty. It cuts through the pretense of congeniality, the collusion of sympathy. The answer seems obvious. But is it? Is it for us? Notice that the man never really answers.

"Sir," he begins. There's the modus operandi of a con artist. "Sir," he says, then lays out his list of grievances. "No one helps me. When the water is stirred up, people push in front of me. No one cares about me. Thirty-eight years and all I got is more of the same."

Jesus question hangs there unanswered: "What do you want?" The sad thing is that the man doesn't seem to think the question really applies to him. It's as if the possibility it carries is too great for him to imagine any more. Healing? Creativity? Freedom? Joy? For *me*? You must be crazy.

Are those possibilities too great for us to claim? Is mystery, risk, grace gone for us? How do you answer Jesus' question, "What do you want? Do you want to be healed?" It's a profoundly religious question. It's a profoundly healing question.

Like this man, too many of us don't consider the question relevant to us. We don't think God actually cares about us or our lives or our healing. If anything, we think God cares only about major things, the sweep of history, the functions of the universe. So we mumble something about miracles of healing not being possible, about new and different options being illusions. Or we assume it's selfish and vaguely immoral to think or risk or live toward what we want.

But Jesus goes down and dirty, and presses us to come clean: *"What do you want?"* It's really a question of identity. Who are you?

In Cormac McCarthy's magnificent novel *All The Pretty Horses*, an older woman, Maria, tells the story of her life to the young cowboy, John Grady. Maria speaks of being sixteen and facing a hard decision: " . . . I knew that what I was seeking to discover was a thing I'd always known. That all courage is a form of constancy. That it is always himself that the coward abandoned first. After this all other betrayals came easily. I knew that courage came with less struggle for some than for others but I believed that anyone who desired it could have it. That the desire for it was the thing itself. The thing itself."[3]

"It is always himself that the coward abandons first. After this all other betrayals come easily."

Maria's words underscore why Jesus question is so powerfully compelling and healing. *"What do you want? Do you desire to be healed?"* It takes courage to answer "Yes" to that question and mean it. We're all veterans of pain of some kind, broken dreams rattling around in us. All of us are stitched by scars.

Walter Brueggemann talks about "the failure of Easter nerve." It's a telling term, isn't it? Since we seldom claim the audacity of the mystery of grace, we close up and shut down. Brueggemann writes, "The Prince of Darkness tries frantically to keep the world closed so that we can be administered. The Prince has powerful allies in this age."[4]

What a chilling image—a closed world where we are administered. A closed world where we, in turn, administer our own lives to manageable objectives. Where's the mystery in a closed world? Where's the celebration? Where's the worship? Where's the wonder of loving what's left to us?

What's left are wounds, yes, but also being alive not dead, touched by wonder, filled with laughter, charged with wild possibilities, summoned to hope and joy. Love what's left to you because it's stunning. It's the kingdom of God.

What each of us has to left to love is our self, at least at first, because it's where the grace that comes by the hard work of art begins. Creativity is putting yourself on the line—"making it," as Alice puts it. It's imagining yourself with all those wild possibilities and churning up the courage to pursue them. Not to claim and risk your possibilities is to abandon your self. Then all other betrayals come easily—especially the betrayal of the mystery of grace.

A very wise person once said to me, "Resentment slowly kills your spirit. If you dare to push through it and choose what is truest about yourself, that's a holy act. Choosing like that is a source of life. It enlarges life places and builds relationships. You become a source of life."

"Resentment slowly kills your spirit." Do we see the man by the pool in that? Or ourselves? Or the possibilities for something different for us and for those with whom we dare to share the art of grace?

Choosing what is truest about ourselves is a holy act. It comes close to what loving ourselves is about. It is what grace enables, what mystery touches on. It is what Easter nerve involves. Courage, then, for that's the beginning of healing and freedom and creativity.

"Do you want to be healed? What do you want?"

There is in each of us a core, a soul, that is a gift of God. Each of us is of great value that is not subject to the hazards of pain, loss, injury, circumstance.

"You got anything left to you to love, anything at all, do it."
Whatever our difficulties are, we have a great deal left to us. Our
being alive. Claim it. Do it!

And that's the second thing Jesus said to the in-valid man,
and to us. It was quick and clean. Do it! "Stand up, take your
mat and walk."

Someone once said, "I didn't fall in love, I rose in it." That's
a great image, isn't it? Falling in love is wonderful, and everyone
should experience the plunge. It's about music, poetry, dancing,
candlelight, all those good things we sometimes think is all that
joy and celebration mean. But everyone should experience *rising*
in love even more. That's about getting up and walking when
it's tough. It's about laughter in the midst of sweat and risk, blisters and battle.

Evelyn Waugh was a writer who got increasingly bitter
with age. He self-righteously withdrew from the world because
he thought the world was going to hell in a handbasket. When
he died, someone observed that "Waugh was offered more love
than he was ever able to accept."

In a way, that's true of all of us, and that's the haunt of
grace. God offers us more love than we usually dare to risk in the
art of living it out. Celebration is a lifetime art. It's about daring
to accept more of that love day by day, and rising in it in whatever way we dare.

Franz Rosenzweig says, "One hears differently when one
hears in doing."[5] That truth is what the art of life is about, what
faith means. I'm not sure we ever really learn the truth by talking, which is a risky thing for a word merchant like me to say.
We do hear differently in doing. That's a real thing!

We find out about prayer by praying, casting ourselves
with disciplined abandon into the silence day by day, listening to
the silence until we hear the love and holiness in it for us.

We learn about God by trusting in the darkness, stepping

out on the promise, walking through the storms and into battle for justice in our homes and neighborhoods, city and world.

We learn mercy by forgiving someone who has hurt us. That doesn't mean walking as if nothing happened and gossiping about whoever offended us. It means confronting those who hurt us, telling them our truth, listening to their truth, working on the relationship for however many lifetimes it takes. We learn mercy by forgiving someone who has hurt us and whom we've hurt as well, if we're honest about it. *"Grace comes by art, and art does not come easy."* One does hear differently in doing. That's a real thing!

On my study wall is a simple silk screen on which are words from a Roethke poem I love:

> Of those so close beside me, which are you?
> God bless the Ground! I shall walk softly there,
> And learn by going where I have to go . . .
>
> This shaking keeps me steady. I should know.
> What falls away is always. And is near.
> I wake to sleep, and take my waking slow.
> I learn by going where I have to go.[6]

". . . learn by going where I have to go." We find our way more by walking than by studying maps. We confirm mystery and "make it" by going on into the always uncharted time and space ahead and daring to fail, if need be. We claim our value by daring to live by what we value, as well as thinking and talking about it.

"Stand up, take your mat and walk." Just that.

Remember, the gospel doesn't say what the man's physical illness was. When he got up and walked, maybe he still had a hitch in his gait, or had one arm hanging useless by his side, or had an eye missing, or his body was still troubled by some shaking that kept him steady, now. And surely, not all his questions were answered. He just squared his shoulders and put one foot ahead of the other and started after a different life. So with us! As Alice said, *"Nobody's asking you to take it. I'm sayin make it, make it."* That's the mystery of grace: We can walk.

The mystery of grace also includes claiming the strength in our wounds and losses. The wonder is that only when we *"stand up, take our mat and walk"* do we make our way back into the human enterprise, which cannot quite go on without us. That's what the church, the gathering of faithful people, is about—not perfection or success but integrity, courage, the art by which grace comes. Faith comes by living faithfully.

"Making it" with what we have left isn't about perfection, it's about integrity, the integrity of living a life that's all of a piece, not split into pieces. The integrity of saying what we mean and then letting our lives mean what we say. Faith is about walking, loving what's left to us and so, hearing differently.

"Mind what's left."

"God does," Jesus is saying when he tells the man, and us, to get up and walk. The gospel also tells us we are loved with more love than we'll be able to accept, unless we rise in love to something like eternal life. That's what this human walk of life is about. God walks with us in the world, an unseen, haunting presence. The mystery and celebration is that we learn by walking where we have to go, and with whom.

And finally, there is the laughter—always the laughter. Alice and Violet laughing as the iron scorches a week's wages away from a poor woman, but the world coming right side up at the same time. And don't you suppose Jesus was laughing, and the man as well, as he rolled up his mat and hitched himself on out of thirty-eight years of fraud, and the world coming right side up again? Don't you suppose he was laughing—at himself being free at last, over the wonder of the world, for the "among us" of God's kingdom?

"*. . . laughter is serious. More complicated, more serious than tears.*"

Of course, we cry. More of us need to learn to do it better, and more often, given the way we treat each other and the world. Tears are necessary, a prelude to doing something about what makes us cry.

Then the laughter. That's a real thing. All the while, the laughter. Every step, the laughter. We laugh in wonder, in delight. We laugh at our foolishness, which gives perspective. We laugh in relief, which gives us strange comfort. We laugh in confidence, not that we will win but that God will, *is* even now, and in God's sneaky way, there'll be no losers—except maybe those who refuse to stand and walk.

Laughter is more serious than tears because in tears we take only the human side of things seriously. In laughter, we take the mystery of God's side more seriously. Indeed, laughter is the truth of taking God more seriously than we take ourselves.

Back when *The Saturday Evening Post* magazine had covers by Norman Rockwell, they also had covers by Richard Sargent. One of Dick Sargent's covers was of a woman in church singing at the top of her lungs, blissfully oblivious to the fact that children were giggling at her and adults were singing somewhere between grimaces and chuckles. The woman's name was Marion Poggenburg. I know, because both she and Dick Sargent were members of a church I once served in New Rochelle, New York.

What it didn't show was that Marion Poggenburg just had a radical mastectomy. She was a large, buxom woman. She joked that her operation "left a lot of me missing." She knew her chances for a cure weren't good, and at first she was depressed. She'd been unable to have children. She'd lost her husband. Now this.

But then, as she put it, "I looked my faith straight in the face, or it looked me straight in the face, and frankly, neither face was all that pretty. But I realized that I had to leave some things up to God, just as God had left some things up to me. Isn't that what love is all about, after all? So it's up to me to get on with living my days, however many there are. The best I can. With all that's left of me."

And that's what she did. Dick Sargent's portrayal of her singing in church was really very typical of her. She was irrepressibly vital. She was the last of the .400 hitters—she hit about 4 out of 10 notes of every hymn. Yet she sang as loudly as she could, even though her vibrato sounded a little like a car with a low battery trying to start on a cold morning. She never finished the verses when everyone else did. So half the last line of every hymn was a Marion Poggenburg solo. She told people that if she didn't have to stuff half her bra with old socks, which "confines my breathing a little," she could sing even better.

She prayed the same way, only faster, as if trying to drag us by the collar to the throne of grace which, I have a hunch, she probably did. There was no way you could come to church and pray, or join in singing the hymns, without leaving feeling better and laughing a little on your way home.

Just before I left that church, Marion took me and my family to what she called her "hideaway," a little place called Pea Island in Long Island Sound. We sat there in the sand, she in her old-fashioned bathing suit, and watched the waves break against the shore. She said, "I want to forgive you for leaving. But, you know, I'll be leaving myself soon. Truth is, I'm as ready to die as to live, and I really believe either means the other, when all's said and done, if you know what I mean. Anyway, I decided months ago, that part's up to God. My part is being ready and doing whichever."

Then she went tromping off into the ocean and began splashing around. I watched her with tears in my eyes. After a few moments, she turned and motioned for me to come in. She was laughing. She shouted, "Isn't this wonderful? Come on. You'll see." I joined her, and started laughing, too. That's how I remember Marion Poggenburg. She taught me something about mystery and celebration I'm still trying to learn.

"Do you want to be healed?"

"Mind what's left."

"Nobody's asking you to take it. I'm sayin make it, make it."

"Stand up, take your mat and walk."

And laugh, for Christ's sake and for ours, for the haunt of grace is with us wherever we walk, even to the end of the age.

~

1. Toni Morrison, *Jazz* (New York: Alfred A. Knopf, Inc., A Borzoi Book, 1992), 110-13.

2. Norman Maclean, *A River Runs Through It and Other Stories* (New York: Pocket Books, A Division of Simon & Schuster Inc., 1976), 5.

3. Cormac McCarthy, *All the Pretty Horses* (New York: Alfred A. Knopf, Inc., A Borzoi Book, 1992), 235.

4. Walter Brueggemann, *Finally Comes The Poet* (Minneapolis: Augsburg Fortress, 1989), 11.

5. Franz Rosenzweig, *On Jewish Learning* (New York: Schocken Books, 1987).

6. Theodore Roethke, 'The Waking," *The Collected Poem of Theodore Roethke* (Garden City, NY: Doubleday & Company, Inc., 1961), 108.

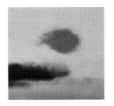

More Than Enough

Someone once said that if someone puts together two words about music, one of them will be wrong. I invite you to remember that as you play over the score of these words.

Many years ago, I quoted in a sermon something about a jazz scene from James Baldwin's novel *Another Country*. A friend liked the quote and used it in a book he was writing, without crediting me for finding it. I was young, and that made me angry, as though somehow the quote belonged to me.

About a year ago, I was in a bookstore leafing through another book and discovered that the author had used the same Baldwin quote and attributed the source to the friend who had borrowed it from me years ago. I was older and smiled. After all, I'd borrowed it from Baldwin, and he was probably writing about an actual incident.

It occurs to me now that the trip the quote took over the years is a little like jazz itself. More deeply, it's a little like life itself. In some way, the quote was something like a riff each of us plays through our lives in the larger concert of human experience. Though the Baldwin quote was a riff of words, not music, three times the quote came around in a different setting. Three times it gave something special to the persons who heard it, to say nothing of all who read it. So now, the piece comes round to me again, or actually, comes round to Baldwin again:

The joint, as Fats Waller would have said, was jumping
. . . And, during the last set . . . the saxophone player . . .
took off on a terrific solo. He was a kid . . . from some insane
place like Jersey City or Syracuse, but somewhere along the
line he had discovered that he could say it with a saxophone
. . . He stood there, wide-legged, humping the air, filling
his barrel chest, shivering in the rags of his twenty-odd
years, and screaming through the horn *Do you love me? Do
you love me? Do you love me?* And, again, *Do you love me? Do
you love me? Do you love me?* . . . the same phrase, unbear-
ably, endlessly, and variously repeated, with all of the force
the boy had.

. . . the question was terrible and real; the boy was blowing with his lungs and guts out of his own short past; somewhere in that past, in the gutters or gang fights . . . in the
acrid room . . . behind marijuana or the needle, under the
smell . . . in the precinct basement, he had received the
blow from which he never would recover and this no one
wanted to believe. *Do you love me? Do you love me? Do you love
me?* The men on the stand stayed with him, cool and at a
little distance, adding and questioning . . . but each man
knew that the boy was blowing for every one of them.[1]

In a thousand ways for me, and I believe for each of us, jazz
keeps asking that question, our question of each other, perhaps,
or of life, or of the universe, or of God: *"Do you love me?"* When
things get twisted out of shape for us, when pain hits, or loss, or
failure, or illness, or the face in the mirror looks back with more
sags and wrinkles than we remember gathering over the years,
and the whole mysterious shebang of it overwhelms us with awe
and questions we feel we're going to drown in, something in us
whispers or screams out, *"Do you love me?"* Do I matter, am I
worth anything much beyond this moment, or to those close beside me who matter so much to me? Something in jazz blows this
riff for all of us.

But the wonder runs even deeper than that. Something in jazz plays the answer, and the answer is "Yes." Jazz, like longing, like grace, haunts us, pours out the ache and agony of our human struggle. It began in the experience of slaves, of wars, of depressions, of betrayals in church and state, of gutters and gangs, and blows in precinct basements and World Trade Towers, and it resonates to whatever our particular versions of the ache and agony of life are. What does it all mean?

"Do you love me? Do you love me?"

Then, around the edges, and in the midst of this wondrous mess, and out of it, comes the joy, the wild or quiet passion, the incredible creativity and hope and faith, the music of the "Yes, I love you."

The "Yes" expresses itself in a thousand other amazing ways, other surprising variations, other irrepressible riffs that are also ours. When asked about jazz, Louis Armstrong answered simply, "What we play is life." Jazz takes the stuff of our common life, the miracles of the ordinary, and plays it with such imagination, and love, that it reminds us it's all uncommon, extraordinary, even sacred, all that about us and our life. And it reminds us of the God who gives life to us, over and over and over again, who is the source of all creativity, and who keeps saying "Yes" to us in one mysterious riff after another. "Yes" is perhaps the one right word about jazz, the word grace shares with jazz, the ultimate word of faith, and of life itself.

A GIFT FOR WHOEVER*

Not long ago, the train I was taking to Hartford, Connecticut, made a stop in New York City. Since it was a thirty-minute layover, I got off the train to stretch my legs and walk around Penn Station. In getting back on the train, I tripped and fell headfirst onto the steel floor of the boarding platform. My first reaction was embarrassment, hoping no one saw me or heard the crash.

I got to my knees. All I could see were a few stars whirling around. I pulled myself to my feet and began looking for my glasses. I spotted them, frames twisted grotesquely, one lens missing. I picked them up, stuffed them in my pocket, and began frantically groping for the missing lens. I found it and pocketed it with the frames.

By then perhaps thirty seconds had elapsed, and I realized there was blood all over my shirt, my pants, and the platform. I pressed my handkerchief to the cut over my eye just as the woman conductor approached. She took my arm, expressed concern, offered to take me for medical attention up in the station. I keep telling her, "No, No, I'm fine. Don't bother. It's nothing."

A second conductor appeared, big as a tackle on the New York Giants football team. He looked at the cut and insisted I

---

* When this reflection was originally presented as a sermon, jazz interludes were offered between each section.

needed stitches. "We'll have a doctor take care of you and put you on the next train north," he said.

"I'm all right. Really," I insisted, blood still streaming down my face. "Head cuts like this bleed a lot. It'll stop soon. Thanks, but I really don't need anything. I'm okay."

A third uniform took shape in the haze. He had a badge. "Look," he said, "I'll call an ambulance, we'll get you taken care of and back on a later train."

I blustered back, "I don't need an ambulance, and I'm not getting off this train. I have to get to Hartford to speak tonight and this weekend. I don't need anything. I'm okay. Thanks anyway."

They led me to the Club Car adjacent to where we were standing and made me sit down. I admit by then I was glad to do that. I was feeling a little dizzy. Someone got me some water. The train was about to pull out. The three good Samaritans hurriedly conferred. The one with the badge finally said, "It's up to you. We can't force you to accept help. But you'll have to sign a release before you leave the train in Hartford." I agreed. They left. The train pulled out. I put on my dark glasses and sat staring out the window all the way to Hartford.

Staring out the window and thinking. What makes me, maybe most of us, so resistant to help, so unwilling to admit and accept the care we need? Whoever wrote the Proverb "Pride goes before a fall" didn't get it quite right. Pride also seems to go *with* a fall and *after* a fall. Not just a physical fall but all the other ways we stumble, hit our limitations, get hurt, experience need, and deny the truth about ourselves. To our own detriment, we choose the illusion of being self-sufficient, in control, independent. Pressing a handkerchief to my eye, I lied through my blood, "I'm fine. I don't need anything." I offer that as a metaphor about most of us.

Staring out the window and thinking. And remembering

something the wonderful priest, teacher, and mystic Henri Nouwen said: "The most difficult thing of all is learning to be loved." Why is it so hard to learn? I suppose love is what we long for most. And yet . . . we proud ones resist. Why?

Staring and thinking. Thinking we resist because love is always a gift. It's nothing we earn, nothing we deserve, nothing we can force, control, win—all those ways, all those things that pride insists we have to do. Earning, deserving is what we're conditioned to do. Falling, failing, flaws are shameful. Gifts are hard for us. Rewards, we're better at. And yet . . . love is always a gift. Some person's love for us. God's love for us all. The only way to have it is to accept it. Simple, and hard, as that.

"The most difficult thing of all is learning to be loved."

And maybe jazz is a good teacher when we pay attention. In an interview, Miles Davis said the secret of jazz musicians is they "don't play what's there, [they] play what's not there."

Who knows for sure what he meant, except all of us get a hint when we listen to jazz. Somehow it's about playing what isn't there, what's more than is visible on the musical score. It's a little like love—maybe more than a little. It's a gift. It's beyond our control, deeper than can be measured, earned, more than a reward. It's just played. It's just heard. It's at least half mystery. Just as is the gospel, and mercy, and grace, and God.

Like love, jazz somehow makes us a bit homesick for something beyond our reach, but it also touches us, sets our feet tapping, our bodies moving, our pulses beating faster, our hearts singing. It brings out of us what our pride denies about us: our need, our hope, our longing for love. For a moment, maybe longer, we accept the gift. And for a moment, maybe longer, life is full, pressed down, shaken together, running over with the gift of it. A gift for whoever will accept it, for what it is.

Staring out the window and thinking, my pride began a meltdown. I realized how too typically sad and foolish I was in denying my need on that train platform in New York—and most of the other places I've been in my life. Sometimes things happen that lead to a meltdown of pride if we dare to let it happen. If we dare to admit our mortality, our frailty . . . and how wonderful it is that we are not only lovers at heart, but beloved at heart, the heart God put into us.

All that weekend I explained how I came by the lovely purple stain around my eye. People said they were afraid to ask because they thought it might be a birthmark. I said, "No, it's not a birthmark. Maybe a re-birth mark, though."

The great jazz musician Wynton Marsalis led a Master Class at the school where my daughter is an administrator. After the young musicians finished their first number, Marsalis asked them what the trumpeter had done during his riff. No one could answer. Marsalis said, "You know, jazz isn't just about playing your own instrument. It's about listening to others. You have to listen in order to know your place in the bigger picture."

Jazz, faith, life, the gospel is about listening. Listening to others, to our deepest longing, to our gifts, yes, but also to our limits, our needs, our mortality. Listening to the intimations of God. Listening in order to know our amazing place in the bigger picture.

A KISS FOR EACH

Not long ago, a doctor friend gave me a copy of Richard Selzer's book *Mortal Lessons.* My friend told me he thought I'd like the book, perhaps find it a book about faith, even God. He was right. This gifted writer and gifted surgeon wrote of an experience that struck me so powerfully, it settled in my soul like a cooing dove:

> I stand by the bed where a young woman lies, her face postoperative, her mouth twisted in palsy, clownish. A tiny twig of the facial nerve, the one to the muscles of her mouth, has been severed. She will be thus from now on. The surgeon had followed with religious fervor the curve of her flesh; I promise you that. Nevertheless, to remove the tumor in her cheek, I had cut the little nerve.
>
> Her young husband is in the room. He stands on the opposite side of the bed, and together they seem to dwell in the evening lamplight, isolated from me, private. Who are they, I ask myself, he and this wry-mouth I have made, who gaze at and touch each other so generously, greedily? The young woman speaks.
>
> "Will my mouth always be like this?" she asks.
>
> "Yes," I say, "it will. It is because the nerve was cut."
>
> She nods, and is silent. But the young man smiles.
>
> "I like it," he says. "It is kind of cute."

All at once I *know* who he is. I understand, and I lower my gaze. One is not bold in an encounter with a god. Unmindful, he bends to kiss her crooked mouth, and I so close I can see how he twists his own lips to accommodate to hers, to show her that their kiss still works.[2]

It puts a lump in your throat, doesn't it? I think of all the people I've known in my life who bear the wounds, the scars that have shaped, and reshaped, their lives in painful ways. That includes everyone I've known, really. I suspect you can say the same about people you've known. You can say it about yourself, can't you? All of us bear burdens, carry wounds, that mark our lives.

So don't all of us wonder if we will always be this way? Since we are human beings, the answer is "Yes." Because something cut us some way. And not just once. We all know heartbreak.

The strange thing is that heartbreak opens us to each other, and to God, in ways that change us. We change more from crises than from intention, don't we? I remember asking my psychiatrist after years of therapy, "John, how long am I going to have these damn problems?"

My problems were painful, and I wanted to be rid of them. I wanted to be perfect. Don't we all? Not being perfect tormented me because I thought that's what I should be. John's answer was liberating.

He said, "All your life."

In that moment I got permission from John to join the human family.

But the incredible thing isn't just that our lives are twisted by wounds of one kind or another. The wonder is that there are those in our lives who kiss us anyway. It's a human kiss, but somehow more than that. Eternally more!

Ornette Coleman once said that "Jazz is the only music in which the same note can be played night after night but differently each time." I think that's one way jazz imitates God. Through lots of people—family, friends, even those we think of as enemies—God keeps twisting her or his lips to kiss our twisted lives so our lives not only still work . . . but still work gracefully. One note, grace, played differently in the lives of each of us. It gives us the pitch on which to start singing our song. It give us a glimpse of who God is.

Like jazz, it's enough. More than enough.

~

1. James Baldwin, *Another Country* (New York: Vintage Books, 1960), 8-9.
2. Richard Selzer, *Mortal Lessons: Notes on the Art of Surgery* (New York: Harcourt Brace & Company, A Harvest Book, 1974), 45-46.

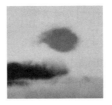

Breaking the Code

Luke 4:16-30

The rankled villagers growl, "Is not this Joseph's son?" Their question cuts to the religious chase. It's a dismissal. Near the beginning of his public life, Jesus goes back to his hometown and visits the synagogue. There he tells people who he is and what he's about. He begins by reading the prophet Isaiah: "The Spirit of the Lord is upon me, because he has anointed me to bring good news to the poor . . . release to the captives." Then he says, "Today this scripture has been fulfilled in your hearing." It's a provocative claim. At least no one dozes off. But the hackles-up citizens can't wait to set Jesus straight. "Don't give us that stuff. We know who you are. We watched you grow up. You're just the carpenter's kid. We know the messiah profile and you're no messiah! So stifle this ridiculous posturing. Don't get out of line and make trouble."

"Is not this Joseph's son?" It's a capsule version of people's response to Jesus from first to last, from beginning to end. And from then to now, because we also know who Jesus is, and isn't, don't we? Ergo, we also know who God is, and isn't, right? Of course. So?

So this. Amidst the flurry of reminiscences written about Jacqueline Kennedy Onassis when she died, the words of Adam Gopnik snagged my attention: "Everything that we Americans did to her tried to turn her into an object—on the night of her death, ABC thought it seemly to run not once but twice the film of her husband's murder—and everything she did was to try to make herself back into a subject."[1]

Gopnik's observation disturbs like a siren in the night. It goes far beyond Jackie O. We are all good at making objects of people. We put each other in pigeon holes, as if we were pigeons. It goes like this: he acts like a man, she reacts like a woman, and there you have it. He's white, she's African American, and that explains it. He's clergy, a social worker, she's a lawyer, a doctor, he's a teacher, a businessman, he makes 125 grand per, she's a welfare mother, so now you know. She's a democrat, he's a re-publican, he's gay, she's divorced, and that's the size of it. In the process of turning others into objects, we do the same to our-selves without realizing it.

"Is not this Joseph's son?" We could be looking out the win-dow or in the mirror when we ask.

We turn ourselves and each other into objects by using a kind of code. We learn the code early. After he had left office, A. Bartlett Giamatti gave a speech in which he said that when he became President of Yale, he was pressured to come up with a policy that would define Yale's mission. One night, crouched in his garage between the lawnmower and the snow tires, Giamatti wrote this memo on university policy: ". . . I wish to announce that henceforth, as a matter of University policy, evil is abolished and paradise is restored. I trust all of us will do whatever is possi-ble to achieve this policy objective."[2]

It's an obvious spoof. But Giamatti clearly meant it as a warning against the growing demand to reduce complex realties into simplistic codes and then applying those codes to every-thing and everyone in our society—such as the deniers of left or right, the diagnosticians for whom all illnesses are similar be-cause all cures are identical, the myopic for whom all the world's pain is simply reduced to their cause, the simplifiers who have boiled life down to a bumper sticker, a T-shirt maxim.[3] These are dangerous trends that impoverish us all.

We all know the codes. We all use them. We use them because they're efficient, time-saving, a quick way to communicate partial truths that are useful. The trouble comes when we begin to take those fragments of truth as the whole truth, or even a basic truth, about each other and ourselves.

"Is not this Joseph's son?"

And there we are with the villagers growling about Jesus among themselves, "Sure, this is Joseph's son. We know the scoop on him, the script to follow in dealing with him." And so they do because they've made an object of him. That makes it easier to dismiss him, to run him out of town in the end. It's all so familiar.

The great Jewish philosopher Martin Buber said we often turn "Thou's" into "its" and live in a world of "I-it" relationships, even in our families. We make objects, "its," of human beings and collude in making ourselves "its" as well. And yet, what's holy in life, what we deeply long for, are I-Thou relationships.

But the concern on my heart isn't just that we make objects of each other. My concern is to keep "it" from happening to us. How do we break the code that reduces us to objects, even to ourselves? What was so striking about Gopnik's reflection on Jackie Onassis was that "everything she did was to try to make herself back into a subject."

As I thought about it, I realized that Jesus always insisted on making himself back into a subject when people tried to make him an object: "good," as the rich man tried to do in Luke 18; or "political revolutionary," as the mother of James and John tried to do in Matthew 20; or "Messiah" as Peter declared in Mark 8. Among other reasons to tell the disciples not to say anything like that about him was his resisting being made the "expected" object, or "King" by coming down from the cross as the jeering leaders challenged him to do.

I believe that's what God is always about, as well, trying to make himself/herself, into a subject, not an object—not an oblong blur, not a philosophical abstraction or First Cause, not a generalized Idea, not an aesthetic icon or a magician to do miracles on cue of the fervently faithful, not any of the ways we tend to make God an object. God becoming a subject is at least part of what the incarnation means. So what could making ourselves subjects mean to us?

~

Before anything else, I believe breaking the code and making ourselves subjects involves claiming our own strange particularities, our own gifts and ground. That's what Jesus was doing there in the Nazareth synagogue—and it's hard to do! Luke's account of it, as well as our own experience, confirms just how hard. To keep making ourselves subjects, we have to resist a lot of pressure to be something we aren't, to do things that aren't rooted in our core. The constant temptation is to act and speak, even think, as if we were only our profession, our work, our race or gender or marital status, or social standing or nationality, or political persuasion—or whatever "it" is—in order to belong, function, get ahead, be "well liked," as Willy Loman put it in *Death of a Salesman.*

I can't tell you how much I dislike being coded as a minister. It shrinks my relationships by defining people's expectations of me and, therefore, their responses to me. If I play that game—and too often I do—I'm an accomplice in the crime of making myself an "it," an object rather than a flesh-and-blood, wondrous yet warted person. We all play that code game because we want to succeed, pay the mortgage, stock the pantry, dress the style, send the kids to camp or college. Of course, we need those things. But how much of them do we need, and at what price? If the price is our soul, if the price is allowing ourselves to ossify into being objects, it's too high.

But there's also a cost in making ourselves a subject again and again and again, dozens of times a day. The cost is a lot of courage. The cost is paying attention to our deepest longing instead of the pitch of hucksters of all stripes. The cost is a willingness to be humiliated, which I believe is what humility really means. The cost is daring to stand our ground against the constant undertow of conformity.

The cost is pitching our tent in the sometimes uncomfortable place of being with others who also keep trying to remake themselves as subjects. They confront, challenge, and support us. They care enough to tell us what they really think and see and mean, and so what we need to hear, not what we want to hear. It is like being Jacob wrestling with the stranger until he got a blessing from him, because that is how we get a blessing and give one in return (Genesis 32:22ff). The cost is being faithful in our living even when our faith is shaky, or small as a mustard seed. I believe that's what Jesus was about, and what he calls us to be about as well.

The choice to keep making ourselves subjects is one of the recurring crossroad choices of life and of faith. Perhaps it is too simple, but only a little, to suggest that the choice is between our real self and gaining pseudo status, between risky freedom and comfortable conformity.

The poet W. H. Auden describes this choice provocatively in his poem "For the Time Being":

SIMEON

. . . by Him [Jesus] is illuminated the time in which we execute those choices through which our freedom is realized or prevented, for the course of History is predictable in the degree to which all men love themselves, and spontaneous in the degree to which each man loves God and through Him {God} his neighbor.

CHORUS

The distresses of choice are our chance to be blessed.[4]

"The distresses of choice are our chance to be blessed."

Mid-life crisis isn't the right term for the turbulence of frustration and anxiety that results in those changes some people make at 40 or 50. The term should be pre-life crisis, and a pre-life crisis can strike at any time from 14 to 44 to 64 to 84. A pre-life crisis is about daring to keep remaking ourselves back into subjects for our own and everyone's sake.

In her book *For Love*, Sue Miller writes of a man named Jack whose wife, Evelyn, suffered a stroke that left her terribly incapacitated. It was a pre-life crisis for Jack. What happened as a result was that he rediscovered himself, and his wife. By holding and touching Evelyn, by giving when there was nothing to get back from her, he learned to love her again, in a different way. There was no obvious gain in it, except living as a subject, seeing his wife as a subject, and exercising the compassion at his core, and the freedom in that.[5]

When you strip it down, life is not first of all about getting things, or getting ahead, or getting anything much. It's about giving. I'm not talking about giving things or money, though if there are too many things we can't live without, we need to have a hard look at that. If we aren't generous, we need to examine what that says about us.

What I'm really calling us to is giving our *selves* by constantly remaking ourselves back into subjects for our own sakes and for the sake of others—and for the sake of God. I deeply believe that's what's involved in loving our neighbors as ourselves.

God has given each of us gifts that are unique to us. Each of us is one of a kind, the only one that will ever live in this time and world with just the constellation of gifts each of us has. Surely we would not have those gifts unless God wants us to claim them and give them, whatever they are.

"The distresses of choice are our chance to be blessed."

So one key choice in becoming a subject is to make our gifts into verbs, to act on them, live them out. Not to risk that is to be an accomplice in the fraud of settling for being an object rather than remaking ourselves back into subjects at least two or three times a day. It doesn't matter what people do with our gifts. What matters is that when we dare to give our gifts, we become a subject not an object for them. In that dare is our freedom.

And in that dare is the option of freedom for others, as well. Our choice for making ourselves subjects gives them that choice. It makes something different possible for them. It's an invitation to others to relate to us subject to subject. Love is more than a meeting of bodies, it is a meeting of souls. That meeting is what we so deeply long toward. When we dare to give our selves to others, we invite others to move toward that meeting with us. We make that choice possible for them, just as Jesus makes it possible for us. For the heart of freedom is not to be afraid to risk moving toward each other.

"The distresses of choice are our chance to be blessed."

Now let's swat the fly buzzing around the edges of what I'm saying. Isn't this about too much self-concern, too much self-preoccupation, too much plain selfishness? Well, it might be and that's a danger. But those things are part of everything we do, and always a danger. But consider something Oscar Wilde said: "Selfishness is not living as one wishes to live; it is asking others to live as one wishes to live." Let that sink in!

Wilde's words seem to be powerful, accurate, full of grace and the gospel. To ask, to manipulate, to try to seduce or coerce others to live as we wish to live is a terrible kind of tyranny. Yet that tyranny is epidemic.

Here's an instance. The Judicial Council of the United Methodist Church has ruled that no United Methodist clergy can perform same gender Covenant Services, nor can any United Methodist Church let its facilities be used for such a service. Clergy can lose their ordination orders if they ignore this rule. That is institutional selfishness. That is to treat homosexual persons as objects when they are as complex and human as anyone else, and often more faithful. That's tyranny.

The way to resist tyranny is to live as we "wish to live," as we most deeply long to live, and so invite others to do the same. It is to keep remaking ourselves into subjects and encouraging others to do so, too. It takes courage to do that. But remember courage is contagious. As a boy I remember my Dad singing with gusto, "Give me ten men who are stout hearted men, and I'll soon give you ten thousand more." I believe it works that way, and that is how change happens.

Of course, there's a cost in making ourselves subjects. There's a cost in treating others as subjects. That's why it takes courage. Maybe the cost will be a loss of popularity or promotion. Surely the cost will be criticism, for many people would rather criticize other's choices and gifts than claim their own. Criticism is easier. I know that. So do you. But there is enormous benefit in being a subject rather than an object.

So Jesus did not back down from his claim of who he was and what he was about. He did not fudge on his claim that "the spirit of the Lord is upon me," that he was a bringer of "good news," a prophet, a healer, a liberator, a fulfiller not an exploiter. He did not shrink under ridicule and threat of rejection. In a desperate effort to make Jesus an object, others tried to make him a dead man. But when the raging crowd tried to do that in Jesus' hometown, they didn't succeed. Even when, at last, people did manage to make Jesus into an object by killing him, making him a dead body, God remade him back into a subject. That's the way of resurrection.

We try to make Jesus an object, an icon, an answer, an idol, a lover of our own specifications, a rubber stamp of our preferences, but God continually surprises us by making him back into a subject.

My good friend Bill Coffin says that Jesus preferred to be rejected for who he was rather than to be accepted for who he wasn't. That is freedom, and the promise of the gospel. Jesus invites and enables us to join him in fighting to remake ourselves into subjects, to claim and live out our particular gifts. He urges us to trust him and step out on the promise of freedom. That is the way faith moves once and again and a thousand times.

~

Another thing involved in breaking the code and being a subject is showing our face, our real face. It's about being present to others, moment by moment. There is a kind of deep security in claiming our own gifts that frees us to really pay attention to other people. We don't have to prove anything, or compete with them, or cut them down to make ourselves look bigger, smarter, better, more important.

When we claim our own gifts, we don't have to do all those subtle, insidious things that make us into an object to put along side other objects, all those things men and women do to each other, or clergy do to each other and parishioners, or doctors to patients, or lawyers to clients, or teachers to students, parents to children, siblings to each other, and on and on.

In the ugly game of comparisons, someone is always wounded and left feeling terribly insufficient. That's the point of the game, isn't it? It's a bad game to be as good at as most of us are. I'm good at it, and I'm ashamed of that because I know, from the losers' side, the pain it causes, and from the winner's side, the emptiness it leaves behind.

The game of comparative insufficiency often operates with a vengeance, even in marriage. Columnist Barbara Ehrenreich writes that in our day, "A spouse . . . is expected to be not only a co-provider and mate, but a co-parent, financial partner, romantic love object, best friend, fitness adviser, home repair person and scintillating companion . . . In what other area of life would we demand that any one person fulfill such a huge multiplicity of needs? No one would ask his or her accountant to come by and prune the shrubbery, or the pediatrician to take out the garbage . . . only in marriage do we demand the all-purpose . . . Renaissance person."[6]

Well, I'm sure it's not *only* in marriage, but it is often in marriage that such demands operate. It's another variation of the code, making each other into objects. The way to break the code is to be present, to show your real face to your partner. To show your face is a metaphor for talking honestly and directly to each other from the heart. It's to negotiate and appreciate each other's unique gifts, even if the shrubs don't get trimmed. That's what it means to be a subject in an "I-Thou" relationship in marriage. Side by side in open sharing not fused in subtle manipulation.

"Selfishness is not living as one wishes to live; it is asking others to live as one wishes to live."

To love our neighbor is to live as we wish to live so we can help liberate others to live as they wish to live. I'm convinced that is one of the things Jesus was about. He struggled to set people free to live, to be subjects with each other and with God. That's why he kept confronting people, holding them accountable to what they said they wanted and believed. That's why he paid attention to all kinds of people, from the lowliest and sickest to the most powerful and wealthy.

We all know people who are trapped in being critical, complaining, cynical, angry, and are not living as they wish to live, no matter how it might look. Often they are people who need attitude adjustments, an enlarged capacity for gratitude, and the courage to risk making life changes. But sometimes people are not living as they wish because the conditions of their lives make it nearly impossible. That could be *partly* our responsibility, especially if we do nothing to address the poverty, disease, exploitation, and despair about which people rightly complain.

Sometimes their complaints become violent, and our reactions become largely vengeful. We dehumanize ourselves and each other. We become objects—enemies, criminals, terrorists, oppressors, righteous warriors, evil ones. In a column in the Israeli newspaper *Yedoit Ahronot*, Nahum Barnea put the matter succinctly: "The terrorism of suicide bombings is born of despair. There is no military solution to despair."

That's a powerful, moral, humanizing truth about the despair of terrorist suicide bombings in the market places and buses and Seder gatherings in Israel and those in the New York World Trade Center and the Washington, D.C., Pentagon. Whatever military action is required, it will not bring a solution to despair. To move toward a solution requires that we remake ourselves into subjects, see others as subjects and invite us all to act accordingly.

To act accordingly would be to take the lead in working together in creating conditions that will overcome poverty, hunger, disease, oppression. Deep down, we all wish to live—long to live—the way God put it in us to live. Whether we call that God "Allah" or "Yahweh" or "Father," the longing in us, and God's longing for us, is to live as subjects together in humility, fairness, respect, justice, and peace in our families and in the family of humanity.

Go back for a moment to what Gopnik said about Jackie O

trying to be a subject rather than an object. A key part of that effort was that rather than insisting attention be focused on her importance and celebrity, "Mrs. Onassis paid new people the infinitely difficult compliment of assuming that the baggage you both brought to the table was of infinitely less importance than the new gifts you might take away from it. Those gifts, for her, included making her own [self] available and undramatic . . . letting a person into her charmed circle . . . "[7]

There it is!

Every one of us has a charmed circle. Showing our real face, paying attention, being less concerned for past baggage than for being open to present gifts, letting others into our circle—which is the circle of grace—is to be a subject, not an object, and invites others to be subjects, too. I believe that's a huge part of what Jesus is and does by showing us that the kingdom of God is in our midst, not in our possession.

～

One last thing involved in breaking the code and making ourselves subjects every day is, instead of praying our hearts out, praying our hearts "in." I believe prayer is a basic way to be a subject with God, and to respond to God as a subject.

When we go about trying to prove or disprove God's existence, or when we talk *about* God rather than *to* God, or when we consider God to be our name for the objective laws that govern the universe, or the impersonal enforcer of moral laws, or the endorser of our causes and privileges, God becomes an object.

Prayer opens us to God as a subject, a "Thou" for an "I" to be in relationship with, to worship with our gifts, to pay attention to with our presence. Prayer is the source of the power to constantly make ourselves back into subjects in a world intent on making us objects. Praying your heart "in" is to resist the tendency to become "heartless" in the frantic, impersonal rush of the world. Prayer is being open to the surprises, the wonder, the grace of an I-Thou relationship with God, dynamic as that relationship can be.

It's not such a solemn, sanctimonious thing, either. In Sue Miller's novel *For Love*, a middle-age woman, Lottie, is having supper with her college-age son, Ryan. Lottie is searching for some kind of healing for herself and her past, including her estranged brother, Cameron, and her own dead mother whose house she and Ryan have been working on together for most of the summer.

Lottie and Ryan sit drinking their beer. Ryan says, "Do you think Uncle Cam is . . . well, dangerous?"

"I don't know, hon. He *is* such a humorless guy, finally."

"What does humor have to do with it?"

"It just does. Believe me, it does."

"That's ridiculous, Mom. What could possibly be funny in this situation?"

"I don't know. I mean, of course, really nothing is. I don't mean that kind of humor, I guess. Just . . . I guess I don't think you can forgive yourself for anything—much less forgive anyone else—if you can't somehow let go of . . . what? The *gravity* of everything? Something like that."[8]

I agree, it is something like that, like the gravity of everything. Certainly religion is serious, but it isn't grave. Yet it seems to exist in a cloud of gravity for too many people who find that almost reason enough to head for the door. At least, I hope *almost*.

Take that day in the synagogue. I imagine Jesus being full of enthusiasm and excitement as he looks at the familiar faces he's known as a boy and announces to them, "Today this scripture [of Isaiah] has been fulfilled in your hearing." Can't you imagine him smiling, even laughing, as he says that? Remember,

Jesus was thirty years old at that moment, not the thirteen- or fourteen-year-old of the villagers petrified perceptions, nor the two-thousand-year-old of our "gentle Jesus meek and mild" re-vised version of him.

Think of the excitement and fun he calls us to join him in having. Think of the fun of being a live subject outside the box of those villagers' dead stereotypes of him, or the fun he has be-ing himself outside the boxes we try to put him in. Isn't that appealing? Think of the excitement of releasing prisoners locked in similar kinds of boxes. Think of the fun of bringing good news to the poor that they are valued by God, and of heal-ing the blindness of people who can't see the gifts they have to give each other. Imagine the fun in setting free people op-pressed by conditions that keep them from living as they wish to live instead of the way others wish, or collude, in making them live. Sound like a good time, a good news time? Then push past the gravity of everything summed up in that dismiss-ive question, *"Is not this Joseph's son?"*

The point I'm after is that there is vitality, excitement, fun in being a subject. There's fun in praying, fun in accepting and giving forgiveness, excitement in I-Thou relationships, excite-ment in the gospel. Someone once said, "God answers prayer in four ways: yes, no, later, and you've got to be kidding." Some-times when I pray, I do hear, "You've got to be kidding." Not a bad way to get perspective. And if we can giggle a little when we realize that sometimes the joke is on us, that sometimes we *are* the joke, then we've inched a little closer to being a sub-ject.

Maybe you've heard the story about the cruise ship that was sinking and the captain yelled, "Anyone here know how to pray?"

One guy stepped forward.

"I do," he said.

"Good," the captain replied. "You pray. The rest of us will put on life preservers. We're one short."

Even so, to live at all and forgive anything, including ourselves, we've got to let go of something like our gravity about everything. We've got to let go of the gravity of ourselves as if the outcome of everything depended on us. Sometimes we lose. Sometimes it's "No" or "You've got to be kidding." And then there's getting on with it, and with God. None of us are objects of fate, victims of a cosmic conspiracy, playthings of happenstance. We are subjects of God who is always trying be a subject to us and to get free of the ways we make an object of God with our debates and dogmas, our disgruntlements and doubts, and our selfishness in asking God to live the way we wish to live.

Prayer is groping our way toward living as we wish to live, as subjects, and to live that way with God the subject. That's maybe more than half of what grace means. The whole thing comes down to an I-Thou relationship with God, with self, with neighbor, with enemy.

A few years ago, *Reflections,* the Journal of Yale Divinity School, carried the reminiscences of women who graduated from YDS before the sixties. Ruth Shinn, a classmate of mine, wrote that our beloved professor, H. Richard Niebuhr, introduced students to theological education by saying, "Here we don't have answers to questions. Here we have great mysteries to explore." I remember Niebuhr telling us that, and I've never forgotten it. His words apply not just to theological education, but to life itself, and to the gospel, and the Christian faith—great mysteries, the haunting mysteries of grace and of God to explore.

Remaking ourselves as subjects with particular gifts is an essential part of that exploration. Relating to other human subjects is another essential part. Prayer is another.

"Is not this Joseph's son?"

Oh my, what a wondrous mystery that question presses on

us. And what a wondrous mystery is the Subject about whom this mystery is asked. So are we invited to be about exploring the wonder of it as subjects—and with our lives.

~

1.   Adam Gopnik, *The New Yorker Magazine,* May 30, 1994.

2.   A. Bartlett Giamatti, *A Free and Ordered Space: The Real World of the University* (New York: W. W. Norton & Company, 1988), 18.

3.   The substance and point of Giamatti's thoughts are found in more academic language in his essays on liberal education in *A Free and Ordered Space.*

4.   W. H. Auden, "For the Time Being," *Collected Longer Poems* (New York: Random House, 1969), 182.

5.   Sue Miller, *For Love* (New York: HarperCollins Publishers, 1994).

6.   Barbara Ehrenreich, "Burt, Loni and our way of Life," *Time Magazine,* September 20, 1993.

7.   Gopnik, *The New Yorker Magazine.*

8.   Miller, *For Love,* 266.

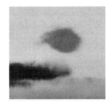

Annex to the Heart

Psalm 145
John 1:43-51

As do other moments of grace, gratitude often comes to me through the back door. For me, the back door hinges began to squeak open when I began moaning about having to go for a week to lecture at an Academy for Spiritual Formation in Minnesota. I flippantly told people I hoped I'd survive the ordeal and those who attended would, too.

I thought of the week as an ordeal because a few years ago I'd had a painful experience leading one of those Academies in California. Yet, in a moment of temporary insanity, I'd signed on to do another, which qualifies me as a bit of a masochist. Then the time of departure was staring me in the face, and all I could see was a gathering of cloyingly saccharin, overly pious, several-degrees-past-pretentious people.

So I went to Minnesota with a chip on my shoulder. I was going to show them, shake them up, shove them in the right direction, then duck and get out of there. But during the week, that chip on my shoulder became an annex to my heart, and the people there moved in and took up residence. They were open, attentive, responsive, willing to go deep, to consider options, see things in different ways. They were profoundly confirming. It was they who showed me, shook me, shoved me in a different direction.

All of us can name a host of things we're thankful for, and I'd guess that most of what we're thankful for are the obvious good things. We do well to take stock of those good things since the list is long. But that's front door stuff, which fits in our hearts without much of a squeeze. Yet it's because of my experience in Minnesota that I want to look at the back door stuff, for which I'm learning to be thankful. I think the most real and deepest gratitude comes through the back door.

~

First, I'm thankful I was wrong about the Spiritual Academy. When I started pondering that fact, it occurred to me that, more times than not, I'm thankful when I'm wrong—even if I don't feel so at the moment. When I'm wrong, it hurts my pride momentarily, but it builds my humility permanently. It pries me open, it stretches me. I am changed more, by far, when I'm wrong than when I'm right. When I'm right, too often that petrifies my point of view.

Someone once said, "Success is the biggest obstacle to creativity and change." That thought haunts me. So I'm grateful that I spend as much time dancing cheek-to-cheek with failure and error as with success and correctness. When I'm wrong and admit it, it puts me in touch with things in myself, in other people, and in the world, for which I have to build an annex to my heart. The annex is needed for those encounters and experiences that don't fit in the well-worn places of my life. And I believe God moves into the annex of my heart with them. I'm very thankful for that when the truth of it dawns on the horizon beyond the familiar.

In John's gospel, Philip is so captivated by meeting Jesus he goes to find his brother, Nathaniel. When Philip tells his brother about Jesus, Nathaniel shrugs and says, "Can anything good come out of Nazareth?" And Philip says all anyone could say to such a question: "Come and see."

"Can anything good come out of Nazareth?"—that run-down-at-the-heels no place, that den of dullards, that swarm of zeros. Sound familiar? Can anything good come out of Minnesota to match up with my compelling religious insights and inerrant moral judgments?

Even more to the point for many of us, can some "mere human being" like Jesus, a marginal peasant preacher-healer who doesn't meet anyone's rational measure, be someone in whom God comes close? Can anything good come out of the unlikely, the dismissible, the unsophisticated, the irritating, the rejects, the disagreeable, the different, the "lesser," the opposition? Could this person who disturbs our certainties and strums our longing be a glimpse of something essential about who God is and what God does?

"Come and see."

When we remember how often we're wrong—and so remember we could be wrong again—only then do we go and see. Only then might we realize that being wrong is less an embarrassment than an epiphany. Such a realization is a visitation from a larger world than we've yet recognized. It's an occasion in which God moves quietly to stretch our spirits and our minds. And it comes holding hands with gratitude and possibilities.

So every day for a week, I came and saw. I lectured and we discussed and wrestled together. Every day we went to morning prayer, and Communion and Evening Prayer, sang the old hymns that can make me, and maybe you, squirm but get into my bones. Every day for extended periods, and every night, we shared silence until that near-death experience became a near-resurrection experience. And the next to the last day, I told the group I'd come in with an attitude and they'd changed it, or God had changed it through them. I was wrong, and thankful I was.

Thankful because, as I told them, they reminded me of what Jesus said in those familiar words in Matthew 25 about being judged by how we treat him when he comes to us as a stranger, in "the least of these," his brothers and sisters. There are many ways to be the "least of these." Yes, of course, the poor, the sick, the oppressed are perhaps foremost among the least of these, and we must remember that. But each of us, in some way, are the least of these as well. That's what makes us brothers and sisters. That's what makes us members of the human family, members of God's family. That's what guards us against our becoming, condescending, self-righteous types who are going to "save" these poor people, whomever we define as being poor because we assume they're inferior—as I pre-defined the Academy people in Minnesota. We'll see Christ in each other if we are open, attentive to different ways of seeing things.

So I saw Christ in those middle-class, educated, not obviously poor, wounded people—like me. All through the week people came to me to talk, to share their stories, asking if we could pray together.

One was a mother whose beautiful teen-age daughter had lupus, which was affecting her brain.

One was a shy woman who shared the story of her daughter's struggle with depression and said she felt helpless except to love her daughter and pray, because even though she loved her daughter with all her heart, she trusted God loved her daughter even more.

One was a young man in agony because he deeply loved his wife and children but had never told anyone, other than me at that moment, that he was gay and didn't know what to do. We talked and prayed, and he asked if he could stay in touch with me and I said I hoped he would.

One was an older man who planned to picket the School of the Americas and knew he would be sent to prison for many months.

One was a woman with cancer who lived alone and wrote music of praise and gave me a copy.

The way the Academy people expressed their faith, the words they used differed from mine, but they were real and so was their faith.

"Come and see."

I was wrong, and so I came to see Christ in those brothers and sisters. And I tell you now, being wrong renewed my near-sighted eyes. I am thankful when I'm wrong because it helps me see God's presence where I hadn't thought to look before, or actually thought not to look.

~

Second, I'm grateful when I'm wobbly. Wobbly is another accessory to the gratitude that sneaks in through the back door. I went to Minnesota to be a leader. I suppose that made it easy to presume I was smart and strong, and needed to be. But really, underneath, I was anxious. When I joked that I hoped I'd survive the week at the Academy, under the bravado I really meant it more than I was willing to honestly admit.

Strange how that goes, isn't it? I don't know who first said, "We always put our best foot forward when it's the other foot that needs the attention," but it's true. I'm good at pretending to be smart and strong when I really feel inadequate and wobbly. I pretend to be sure and self-sufficient when I really need help, challenge, correction. I think we're all good at pretending like that when we really need and long for each other's honest presence, each other's thinking and prayers. I really felt wobbly when I left for the Academy. I wasn't at all sure if I could do what I thought had to be done there, since I didn't see myself as any kind of expert in spiritual formation.

But God is sneaky. One night, a clergyman who attended

the Academy came to me to talk about what I was saying about integrity and being authentic. Earlier, when we were having lunch together, he'd told me that he'd been in an accident and his legs had been damaged. Subsequent surgery for cancer worsened his condition, and it had progressed until he faced losing all use of his legs. Now he got around in a wheelchair, though at times he could negotiate a little with crutches. He'd been forced to retire in his early fifties because of his disability. I asked him if he was angry about his condition, and he replied, "No." But as he said it, trying to smile, his face and his attitude was pinched.

Now, two days later, he wanted to talk and to pray with me. So we did. He told me he longed to be more authentic and honest, but thought it wasn't Christian. He thought he should be strong, optimistic, and brush aside his disability and his feeling of being weak. But what I'd been saying at the Academy made him realize that was phony. When he told me that, I confessed that I was often phony, too. He looked relieved and reached for my hand.

He went on to tell me he really was angry. Then he said, "The funny thing is that when I say that, either out loud or to myself, I feel a lot of energy moving in me. I feel freer. Do you really think God can take me being angry?"

I asked him, "Can *you* take you that way? I don't think it's God who has trouble with your anger. My guess is God will help you use it."

I asked him what he wanted to do. He talked a long time about wanting to establish an inter-faith, inter-church spiritual advisory center for people with all sorts of disabilities. Not just physical but mental and emotional disabilities as well. I told him it seemed to me he was uniquely qualified to take a shot at it, if he could be okay about his own disability. I hunched out my next words: "Maybe that's what the energy in you is about."

His face lit up. "You think so? Is that what you meant when you said God will help me with it?"

I said, "I'm not sure exactly what I meant. You're the one who sees the connection. I'd say, 'Go for it' and see what happens. I do believe God will be in it with you." We talked some more, then prayed together in a kind of wobbly, stammering way.

The next day, the man volunteered to give the meditation for our communion service. He used his crutches to get to the pulpit, and then he hung on to support himself. He began by talking about how our society is all about being strong, being self-sufficient, doing things for ourselves and not asking for help, as if that were demeaning and inhuman. He said his disability had only intensified his dislike of asking for help. So he tried to be self-sufficient and despised himself when he couldn't be. He talked about the macho ideal being the norm, even for women. "It's all about being tough, powerful, fearless, and smart. Weak people are discarded, despised, rejected."

Then he talked about Saint Paul asking God to take away a thorn in his flesh. Instead, God said to Paul, "My grace is sufficient for you, my power is made perfect in weakness" (2 Corinthians 12:9). "Now I'm learning that's what the gospel is about," he said gripping the pulpit. He went on to describe what that was beginning to mean for him, and his dream of starting a spiritual advisory center for disabled people. We knew he wasn't talking just about himself, but about all of us, about everyone.

Disabilities come in many forms. I think of the arrogance and terrible isolation of my compulsion about perfection. I rail against my limitations until I am worn out, and wear others out in the process. Perfectionists drive everyone crazy, as I understand perfectly. I recall once saying to a friend, Carl, that I'd always been taught that whatever I did, even if it was digging a ditch, it had to be "the best." Carl said, "You can't do or be the best at much, or much of the time. I tell my kids sometimes good enough is okay. Getting a C in school is okay."

I almost cried when he said that. Because he's right. We can't do or be the best at everything, or even very much, or maybe in anything. Macho is phony. Those "No Fear" T-shirts cover hearts that know better. Self-sufficiency is a fantasy. *"My grace is sufficient for you, my power is made perfect in weakness."* It takes courage to admit weakness, but courage is the tap root of faith.

"Can anything good come out of Nazareth?" Can a man with a few scraggly followers, and with nail holes in his hands and feet, overthrow Rome, change the course of the world, give abiding meaning to lives through the ages?

"Come and see."

Can anything good come out of you with your weaknesses and limitations? The gospel says, "Yes," if you accept them and throw them in the pot with all the rest of us and our weaknesses and limitations: husbands, wives, kids, all the disabled in the neighborhood, and the welfare moms, the addicts, the homeless, the jobless, the strangely deprived rich, the isolated macho pretenders, all the rest. Do what you can, and that's commitment. Give what you have and are, and that's courage. Then it's about God, and that's faith, hope, trust. It's about grace being sufficient, power working through weakness, and through us.

I'm thankful when I'm wobbly . . . and I'm getting wobblier. Then I can really pray, and then I can let people into my life, and then I can put the burden of pretense down. Then I'll keep adding annexes to my heart to let in other people in whose weakness God is at work, as God is at work in mine. There's no other explanation for any of us. Not really. Build your own annex, and we'll all come in with God.

Permit me this quick aside. Once again, the world seems locked in a terrible, terrifying power struggle. Israel and Palestine slip in each other's blood toward a war of incredible destruction for both sides and the whole Middle East. Everyone knows the only way to peace is for both sides to compromise and to accept each other and live together as two neighbor states. The question is, which will be wobbly in public and move toward building an annex for each other?

There is a war on terrorism underway at the behest of our beloved country. It's a necessary war but surely within limits. The question is, how will it be fought? Only with military force? Only by bombing Hussein out of power and Iraq into misery? Sometimes my lower angels fly to that drum beat. But if we do that, then what? Who wins, who loses, and what is lost or won?

Those are the tough, inescapable moral questions when we get past the first impulse for revenge and second for safety. There is a spiritual, faith dimension to everything, including our response to terrorism.

Surely any war against terrorism must also be a war against poverty, disease, exploitation of the weak by the strong. It's easier to obsess about evil than it is to imagine what it would mean to be good as we see it in Jesus or other great leaders, such as Moses or Isaiah or Gandhi or Mohammed. Just that kind of imagination is a dancing partner of faith. So as a people we need to recognize our own wobbliness. Maybe we need to build an annex to our national heart so it will hold not only Americans but humanity. Maybe admitting our limitation, our need for a true global village isn't such a bad foreign policy. There are people in Israel, and Palestine, and even in this country, who advocate for it. Maybe they, too, are accessories squeezing through the back door. Whether or not we let them in or join them, I, for one, am thankful for their squeeze.

$\sim$

Third, and last for now, I'm thankful when I wonder. Wrong, wobbly, wonder. They make a curious combo. Yet, they're all back door stuff that leads to building an annex to the heart because none of them fits easily into our customary living spaces. Wonder comes with gratitude through that back door.

A cartoon in *The New Yorker* showed a couple of middle-aged, sagging-shouldered guys walking down the street carrying brief cases. One of them says to the other, "I'm at the point where I find mixed messages reassuring." Don't you love that? It is reassuring in this world, where so many people, on so many sides of anything, claim to know the absolute truth about everything. I suppose you could go in a dozen different directions with that cartoon. But try this one: Mixed messages, rather than absolute ones, signal that the world is a mysterious place. That more is going on in it than we know. That there's more to truth than we know. That there's more to God than we know. And there's the wonder!

Jewish leaders once asked Jesus if it was lawful to pay taxes to Caesar. The question was a trap to embarrass and discredit him. The Jewish people despised Caesar for occupying and oppressing their country. Yet open opposition meant severe Roman reprisals. Whatever answer Jesus gave, he'd be in trouble, either for supporting Caesar or advocating rebellion. What did Jesus do? He gave a mixed message. He showed them a coin and asked whose image was on it. The answer was Caesar's. So Jesus said, "Render to Caesar the things that are Caesar's and to God the things that are God's." That's a mixed message, not an absolute one. It leaves us to make our own decisions.

The coin of the realm, then and now, belongs to Caesar. So render to Caesar, that is, to country, to society, the things that are rightfully theirs, and be grateful for the benefits they give us in return.

That leaves God. What do we render to God? Well, whose image do we bear, you and I? From page one, the Bible is clear about that. We bear the image of God. What, then, do we render to God? What else but ourselves. But how? When? Where? Ah, mixed messages and wonder.

Here's the heart of it: It's an awesome thing to be a human being! It's a wonder to know that whatever happens in and to this universe, we are part of it and will always be part of it. It's stunning to know that what we are, what we decide, what we do, is a factor in the continued unfolding of creation. So it is profoundly awesome to realize that there's more going on in this world than we know, or than anyone else knows. We are free to do new things. And certainly God is. So the unknown isn't just about things we don't know yet, it's about things that are unknowable to us mortals. Unknowable to anyone! Not scientists or preachers or politicians or economists or poets or prophets or artists or logicians or rationalists, or whoever. No one knows all, or much, of what's going on in this world, in this creation, in these hearts. We live in and with mystery, and so, with wonder.

Aristotle said that life begins in wonder. He didn't go far enough. Life begins in wonder and *continues* and *ends* in wonder. Most creative things begin and continue in wonder. Poet James Dickey suggests that poets love more intensely, more vitally than other people. Maybe so, since wonder runs up and down poets' spines. But so does it run up and down the spines and within the hearts of people of faith. We are well acquainted with mystery all around and at the depths.

The other thing Dickey said was a quote from his grandmother: "He who ever strives upward, him we can save." I'm not sure what his grandmother meant by that, but I certainly think it applies to poets who, in trying to get something down on paper, strive upward toward words of power and insight that open and lift and surprise us in ways that change how we are in the world.

Even so, people of faith strive upward in a similar way. In fact, I believe all people strive upward, one way or another in some kind of faith, admitted or not. It's a human thing, and most deeply a faith thing. Striving upward is what our deepest longing is about. It's about being saved, made whole, reconciled to each other and God. Striving, not to get ahead, not to get on top, but to reach toward God. That's what it means to pray, to worship, to trust, to risk, to engage each other beneath the surface.

I risk sharing my story "beneath the surface" because I keep going back to it as a hinge moment in my life. It's my very close brush with suicide years ago. I'd prayed and prayed about my depression and anxiety but to no avail. I despaired of God and couldn't see past the darkness. But in the middle of the night I'd decided to end my life, my little four-year-old son padded down the stairs, came over to my lap, hugged me, and went to sleep. I began to cry. I realized that, in some mysterious way, my prayers were answered. I believe such indirect, roundabout ways are God's preferred way to answer prayers. In mysterious ways, we may be answers to each others prayers but never know it.

I told the people at the Academy this story. I went on to say that I believe even if I had committed suicide, God would still have answered my prayer. God isn't limited by our time. Most of us think God only answers prayers some way that fits our categories, the ways we know things happen. Then there are those mixed messages, those multilayered events and experiences full of wonder, of questions, and so of decisions of what we will trust about life. What seems to me unquestionable is that there are more mysterious things going on than we can know or imagine.

So the story goes on. A few days after I came home, I got an e-mail telling me that the teen-age son of one woman, I'll call her Rose, who had been at the Academy, had committed suicide on the Friday night she returned from that week away. Rose had given me a book of poems she'd written about children, inscribing it with gratitude for our time together. Now her son, I'll call him Mike, was dead by suicide. I was stunned. Grief flooded in. I cried as I groped for words to write to Rose.

Two days after I heard about Rose's son, I got an e-mail from another person I'll call Alice. She also attended the Academy and was close to Rose. Alice wrote me about a vision she'd had the night Rose's son killed himself, though she hadn't gotten that news yet. On the night she came home from the Academy, she had a vision of me standing in the auditorium of the retreat center with a noose dangling over my head. Then she was walking down a long, stone-walled corridor, feeling like she was walking toward the crematorium at Auschwitz. Fire began to rise out of the floor, then it turned to clear water, and flowed out like a river. She sensed that God was crying, and she longed to comfort him.

Alice was sure God wanted her to do something, but she didn't know what. It was after midnight, but Alice walked downstairs where her own thirteen-year-old son was watching television. She told him of her vision and asked if he'd ever thought about suicide. He answered no. Even though it was late, she called a friend she worked with who had been talking about taking his life. Alice explained her vision and talked with her friend for nearly half an hour. He was very grateful for her call and for reaching out to him because very few people did that.

On Sunday morning, Alice heard the news of Mike's suicide. She wrote:

I called Rose Sunday evening. I really felt God leading me to share my vision with her, Ted, so I did. She was so thankful. She felt it was an affirmation of the words you shared at the retreat about your own thoughts of suicide. She had been clinging to those words, especially when you spoke about how you felt God would have honored and used your suicide within the sovereignty of His will. I am so amazed at how God connects us together, how God uses every-thing for his purposes. I cannot begin to understand the how and why of it all. Simply knowing I, you, Rose, all of us are part of God's plans brings peace and awe, doesn't it?

God bless you my friend,
Alice

"*I cannot begin to understand the how and why of it all. Simply knowing . . . all of us are part of God's plan brings peace and awe, doesn't it?*"

Yes, it does. At least sometimes it does. Enough times. More than enough times. Squeezing through the back door. Enough times to keep building annexes to our hearts just to hold a little of the sneaky grace of God and our strange brothers and sisters of the human family.

Sometime soon go to your back door and think about that. Then lift a prayer of gratitude for the wonder of it all.

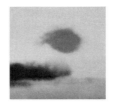

New Rules of Engagement

Matthew 1:18-25

He threw away his reputation as a good man by marrying a fallen woman.

That's one of the little clues to the large wonder of Christmas, and of life. To sense the power of it, revisit the story. Joseph and Mary are engaged but, as Matthew delicately puts it, they have not lived together. So when Mary turns up pregnant, Joseph sees no option but to break off with her if he is to maintain his standing as a righteous man. By getting pregnant as an unmarried woman, Mary has shed her virtue and become an outcast. According to religious law, she's done something for which she could be stoned to death. So, despite his concern for Mary, Joseph plans to disavow her. He feels driven to it by his wounded pride and by what has been drummed into him about what society, and God, required of him.

Then something happens to upset the world for Joseph, and forever. An angel speaks to him, in a dream, no less—and no more. He's haunted by a message in intimations and nudges squeezing in from another world through the cracks in this one. As always, we have to squint our eyes and cock our ears to catch it. The angel fluttering through Joseph's dream tells him not to be afraid to take Mary as his wife, that she's pregnant with Jesus, who will save people from their sins. What's a person to do with that kind of news? What would you do? Run and hide? Or turn and risk? Joseph turned and risked. And a different life began.

"Do not be afraid!" That's nearly the whole meaning of Christmas and the gospel.

Do not be afraid: God is doing a new thing.

Do not be afraid: It's the only way you can have good will toward anyone.

Do not be afraid: It's the basis for new rules of engagement.

Start with the obvious truth that we are all connected. That's the way God put the world together. What happens to any of us affects all of us, like it or not. Many people don't like it, and many don't acknowledge the connection. Even so, the inescapable truth is that everything and everyone on earth is connected. That's the ecosystem of life. Connection is a given.

But engagement is a choice. The choice is whether or not to make connections vital, not just formal; intimate, not superficial; sustaining, not empty.[1]

By now all of us are at least somewhat familiar with Ntozake Shange's marvelous choreopoem *for colored girls who have considered suicide when the rainbow is enuf.* The girls are identified by the different colors they wear as they move in a kind of dance, sharing their experiences of relationships in which they felt exploited, isolated, frustrated, and angry. Near the end, the lady in blue says something that probably puzzles us at first:

> I used to live in the world
> really be in the world
> free & sweet talkin
> good mornin & thank you, & nice day
> uh huh
> i can't now
> i can't be nice to nobody
> nice is such a rip-off
> . . . is just a set-up"[2]

Engagement is a choice against the rip-off. Engagement involves pressing beyond shallow niceness and congeniality, agreement and pretense, to more honest and deep relationships. It is to seek fairness for ourselves and for others. It is to talk to others, rather than talking about them. Engagement is about building trust between each other by saying what we mean and meaning what we say. Without trust, love shrivels and compassion twists into manipulation. Engagement involves honestly sharing truths about ourselves, our thoughts, feelings, and experiences, and inviting others to share their truths with us. That is hard to do but infinitely worth it because it empowers us to find new, larger truths together.

Engagement takes courage, which is half of what faith is. It involves taking risks. By daring to engage each other, we make something different possible between us, and within ourselves. When we honestly share the hard truths we keep hidden in an attempt to be "nice," something deeper, something more healing and redemptive opens up for us that our pretense has kept closed down. Engagement is what Jesus was about. That's why he was harder on hypocrites than on prostitutes, thieves, and tax collectors. Hypocrisy and pretense close things down, mistake congeniality for love, and shrink the possibilities for the abundant life that Jesus urges us to claim for ourselves and each other.

So Joseph dreams, as we all do. In many ways, our dreams and his are alike. We also dream of loving and being loved. We dream dramas of finding a deeper meaning for life, of escaping the demons, of laughing and playing together. In Joseph's dream, the angel tells him not to be afraid to heed the longing in him to move from the empty outskirts of his life into the bustle and excitement and sacred struggle at the heart of things, and of himself.

In some way don't you suppose our dream angels are telling us the same thing: *Do not be afraid.* Listen to your deepest longing for love, for meaning, for relationships that are deep, trusting, satisfying, challenging, and joyful, for a world of justice and peace and beauty. In a haunting way, our dreams call us to engagement, to move from the outskirts to the center of our lives.

The mystery is that while grace engenders engagement, engagement enacts grace. Engagement, then, is our response to Jesus' haunting promise that the kingdom of God itself is *among* us or *between* us. It is not the possession of anyone but is found in our relationships with each other and all God's creation. Healing, justice, forgiveness, peace reside in whether and how we engage each other.

The haunting word of the angel in the dream had it right: "Do not be afraid . . . [Jesus] will save his people from their sins." God's love isn't about endorsing our status, or propping up our self-esteem, or defending our privileges, or sticking a seal of approval on our comforts. It's about saving us from our sins. What does that mean? The condensed answer is that it means calling us out of the pretense and pride and hypocrisy we hide in. There is a real toughness in grace. I believe Jesus demonstrates, and calls for, new rules of engagement.

Not long ago, two people at a retreat I helped lead gave me a sheet of paper with the heading "The Invitation" by Oriah Mountain Dreamer. The words touch on at least a part of what engagement and grace are about:

It doesn't interest me what you do for a living. I want to know what you ache for, and if you dare to dream of meeting your heart's longing.

It doesn't interest me how old you are. I want to know if you will risk looking like a fool for love, for your dream, for the adventure of being alive . . .

I want to know if you have touched the center of your own sorrow, if you have been opened by life's betrayals or have become shriveled and closed from fear of further pain. I want to know if you can sit with pain, mine or your own, without moving to hide it or fade it or fix it.

I want to know if you can be with joy, mine or your own, if you can dance with wildness and let the ecstasy fill you to the tips of your fingers and toes without cautioning us to be careful, to be realistic . . .

I want to know if you can live with failure, yours and mine, and still stand on the edge of the lake and shout to the silver of the full moon, 'Yes!'

It doesn't interest me to know where you live or how much money you have. I want to know if you can get up, after the night of grief and despair, weary and bruised to the bone, and do what needs to be done to feed the children.

It doesn't interest me who you know or how you came to be here. I want to know if you will stand in the center of the fire with me and not shrink back."[3]

Surely something like that is what Joseph heard. Don't be afraid to engage life, yours and others. Don't be afraid to take Mary as your wife, to take risks, to do battle for what you believe at your core. Don't be afraid to battle for love, for honesty, for intimacy, for mercy, for justice, for integrity. Don't be afraid to move out of the box that can become a coffin. Life isn't about innocence, it's about engagement, and Jesus lived by those new rules of engagement. That's what Joseph's dream, his angel, was telling him—and us. So Joseph threw away his reputation as a good man and married the fallen woman. He, and we, know more deeply the grace of God because he did.

As a person who has gone through the pain of a divorce, I've learned the critical difference between connection and divorce. Through the years of our marriage, Dory, my former wife, and I were connected but not engaged. There was more image than reality in our marriage, more the concern to be seen as right and blameless than to be honest and engaged. I tried to live the ideal of what my parents expected, what the church expected, what society expected. I couldn't do it. It led at last to my emotional and spiritual breakdown.

I didn't risk engaging Dory nor, I think, did she risk engaging me. We avoided and denied and pretended. We retreated from each other. We fought but didn't talk, blamed but didn't listen, or speak our truth, or share our hopes and disappointments or our selves.

When the divorce happened, my grown kids were angry with me most about my pretense. It distanced me from them as well, as they were growing up. My kids were burdened by an ideal I pretended to be. I wanted to be seen as good and innocent, but wasn't, could never be, because only God can be. My pretense was wrong. It hurt other people, and it hurt me. Out of my fear I lashed in and I lashed out. I was connected but not engaged.

Since then, from therapy, from my kids, from my deepest longing and dreams, and from my wife, Jan, I've learned about engagement. Since then, I've heard and heeded the angel. It isn't about innocence or goodness. It's about not being afraid, or less afraid, to come out of hiding. It's about being human, not angelic or demonic. Jesus came to save people from their sins. Saved to get engaged and to understand something of the depths and mystery of God's grace.

The incarnation we celebrate at Christmas can be grasped as one of God's unique ways of engaging with us. "And the

Word became flesh and lived among us . . . " (John 1:14). No longer above the fray, but *in* it, in heart of the human struggle, in all the messy, dusty, rocky, boney, fleshy, bloody, gutsy, sweaty, confronting, loving, beauty, and wonder of it. Engagement—not innocence, not idealizing, not niceness but *engagement*—is what Jesus was about and calls us to move toward. When we join the fray with him, we discover what grace and mercy and healing and reconciliation and abundant life are about.

Saving Private Ryan is a soul-shaking movie.[4] Even if you haven't seen it, you'll get this point. There's a timid, seemingly cowardly American soldier, Corporal Upham, who keeps avoiding being involved in the ugly business of the war, or being engaged with the other soldiers in his small squad. I think Corporal Upham was trying to hold on to his innocence. But which of us is really innocent in this fallen world? Innocence is an illusion. And yet it's such a powerful illusion; it drives us to blame others for what's wrong in the world, or in our own lives.

Even in the midst of the terrible war, Corporal Upham clings to "the rules" as though they will keep him safe and innocent. His fear transposes into self-righteousness. He acts like a non-combatant, which he is not. He and the others in his squad are sent behind the Nazi lines hours after the invasion at Normandy. They are to find and bring back to safety Private Ryan, a paratrooper who jumped into Normandy to blow up crucial bridges.

At one point, Upham and his little squad of American soldiers come upon a German radar station and try to take it out. One of their unit is killed in the fight, and, in turn, they take a German soldier prisoner. The others want to shoot the prisoner because it would be very dangerous to take him along as they move around behind enemy lines. But Upham argues that "it's against the rules" to kill a prisoner. So reluctantly, Captain

Miller lets the German prisoner go. The other soldiers in his squad are dismayed because their lives are at stake if the German soldier runs to warn his buddies.

Later, that same German soldier turns up leading a battalion of Germans and, in another encounter, he kills one of the squad of American soldiers while Upham quivers nearby, doing nothing to engage in the fight.

But finally Upham gets the message. He finds the courage to be engaged. He joins the fray. In one encounter he shoots the German soldier. He's less afraid. He comes to "the knowledge of good and evil," so to speak.

Upham's obsession to be only innocent and good was the source of his pretense. It was a weakness that endangered and hurt the others. Upham denied the reality of a power in himself and around him that the rules don't touch, can't touch, a power that twists the rules for its own purposes. Call it sin, or evil, or tyranny. Whatever we call it, it's real. It's in the world. It's in us all.

It was only when Corporal Upham, like Joseph, accepted that reality and got engaged in dealing with it, that he seemed to stop being so afraid. I would go so far as to suggest the radical view that Upham's spiritual life, his spiritual depth and wholeness, began when he risked engagement in a less-than-perfect, east-of-Eden world, rather than trying to maintain the illusion of innocence. Isn't that what Christ did? I think so!

Go just a bit deeper: The "good" that the rules supposedly uphold is often undone by the persistent self-serving and self-deception worming through our claims to be good, even as we routinely try to tilt the rules to our advantage. That is always the danger of good people, like Joseph before his dream, like some of us, like me. Our version of the good replaces God. And yet we're often, maybe usually, afraid because the world is both more cruel than we can control and more beautiful than we can resist.

So here's the mysterious part, the grace part of it. God, the ultimate "good," does not always abide by the rules either. That's what Jesus' birth and life, crucifixion and resurrection are about. They are revelations of God acting, engaging to break the rules of lesser goods, as well as of corruption and death. By his engagement with people, Jesus did miracles that went against the "rules" of madness, sickness, storms, and religious powers. Don't you suppose that's why he was so upset with the hypocrisy of people who limited goodness to the keeping of rules, maintaining their image of innocence while their spirits atrophied? Risk of engagement is based on grace, not on innocence.

Rules are a good thing as far as they go, but they do not exhaust the possibilities for either goodness or evil. We're haunted, nudged to imagine and respond to what lies beyond the bounds sometimes. In both directions. And there is Joseph, throwing his reputation and caution to the winds and engaging with Mary in a new way, and thwarting Herod's plan to kill Jesus along with the other babies in that horrific slaughter of the innocents in Bethlehem.

Christmas, God's invasion of human history, Jesus' birth, has nothing to do with fantasies of innocence. It's about engagement. Too often the call of Christians to conversion seems to be about a conversion to innocence. But it's really a conversion to responsibility, to engagement with whatever dehumanizes, demeans, oppresses people.

"Do not be afraid."

"I want to know if you will risk looking like a fool for love, for your dream, for the adventure of being alive."

Will you risk engaging your self? First that. Engaging your self is a two-way street running from inside out and outside in. It involves taking the risks of trying something different in your relationships with others in the family, the marketplace, the workplace. Those risks can be occasions of self-discovery and

empowerment. But it also involves honest prayer, soul searching, quietness, reflection.

In the conclusion to "The Invitation," Oriah Mountain
Dreamer writes,

> It doesn't interest me where or what or with whom you
> have studied. I want to know what sustains you, from the
> inside, when all else falls away.
>
> I want to know if you can be alone with yourself and if you
> truly like the company you keep in the empty moments.[5]

Even so, I've learned that being sustained inside, liking the
company I keep in the empty moments, isn't about my goodness, my wisdom, my achievements. At least it isn't about those
things all the way down, though you and I claiming our gifts is
part of it.

But more, it's about battling for our integrity, our honesty,
our soul. Tucked in among Annie Dillard's treasury of incredible
insights is a description of an Advent Mass where the organist
couldn't find the opening hymn, acolytes blundered in lighting
candles, a number of strange requests from the congregation
were part of the prayers.

Just as Dillard was on the verge of bursting into laughter,
the priest included this request in his prayer: " 'For my son, that
he may forgive his father, we pray to the Lord.' 'Lord, hear our
prayer,' we responded, chastened." Dillard goes on: "Week after
week, we witness the same miracle: that God is so mighty he can
stifle his own laughter . . . Week after week, Christ washes the
disciples' dirty feet, handles their very toes, and repeats, It is all
right—believe it or not—to be people. Who can believe it?"[6]

Careful now, that's God's first question of us, as it was of
Adam and Eve, and Moses and the Israelites, and the disciples
jockeying for special privilege, and everyone down through the

years. *Who can believe it?* Maybe the father who sought his son's forgiveness in that morning Mass. Christmas, like Jesus washing the disciples' feet, says, "It is all right to be people, to be human." Then comes that haunting, gracious question: *Can you believe it?*

Why that question? Because to be human is to be less than God but more than animals. It is to live in the tension of being both spiritual and physical. When we posture in any guise of proud self-sufficiency, or of indulgent self-degradation, we deny our limits and decline our gifts. We waste resources of minds, hearts, relationships. We become stuck in hypocrisy. We spurn our humanity. Yet how many times a day, or a week, or a life-time, do we do that?

To risk engaging ourselves is to wrestle our humanity out of those denials. The wonder is that we do that wrestling best when we do it together. The wonder is that such wrestling is the heart of relationships and the web of community. We don't fool God by trying to fool ourselves. When we give up such foolishness, we'll love ourselves and our neighbors better, and our honesty and integrity will sustain us in the empty moments. And our prayers and our lives will deepen. That's part of what the new rules of engagement are about.

Then there is the risk of engaging with others and for others. Oriah Mountain Dreamer's question, *"I want to know if you will stand in the center of the fire with me and not shrink back,"* is close to the core of it. Faith isn't about staying on the shallow end of life or the fringes of battle against injustice and oppression. It's about being in the center of the fire where our brothers and sisters are. It's about doing what Luther thundered, "Love God and sin on *boldly*." Sin, because everything about us is tainted with a self-interest we can't escape. But sin boldly. Boldly means being aware of our shadow side yet acting ". . . with firmness in the right as God gives us to see the right," as Lincoln so beautifully framed it,[7] trusting God can still do something with us that benefits others and brings about God's own purposes.

What would happen in your family if you really engaged each other, really spoke honestly, really listened carefully, really challenged as well as credited each other? That's how trust begins and fear eases. Unless there's trust, love is a sham.

What would happen in this world if we dared to engage it more compassionately, demanded better schools, better salaries for teachers, adequate health care for low-income working families, serious efforts to stop global warming, water pollution, an end to poverty in the next hundred years, as the National Council of Churches in Christ in the USA is advocating—to name just a few issues that challenge our humanity and, if met, would do more to end terrorism than all the high tech military weaponry combined?

In the Sunday *New York Times Magazine*, Max Frankel ended one of his columns with these words: "Just as we now wonder how otherwise enlightened people could trade in dark-skinned bodies or demand and accept female subservience, future generations are bound to marvel at how so many of their forebears could routinely feast while others went hungry, or how some ancestors could amass fortunes while others went begging. Like slavery and male domination in their time, the inequalities of our day are justified even in the most progressive circles as not only tolerable but also actually essential to economic growth and social harmony."

Are they really essential? Are those "rules" set in concrete? Are economic incentives the only, or primary ones, or is justice, the welfare of everyone, even more compelling? Never mind that we may be born into circumstances of privilege, as most of us are. The issue is, will we employ our privilege to engage the world on behalf of justice for all?

"I want to know if you can get up, after the night of grief and despair . . . and do what needs to be done to feed the children."

There's the battle. Good rules getting overturned for better ones. That's the haunt of the dream, the nudge of the angel. *Do not be afraid.* Jesus saves the people from their sins. God's grace is deep and empowering. That's what the new rules of engagement are about.

And, finally, what about engaging with Christ? I wish I had the capacity to speak more clearly about this. I think of the great prophetic teacher and social activist Reinhold Niebuhr, who lived out his vision of what he called "Christian realism." But late in his life he wrote this: "I have come to realize that it is possible to look at the human situation without illusion and without despair, only from the standpoint of the Christ-revelation . . . I have come to know . . . that only in the 'simplicity of the gospel' is it possible to measure the full 'dignity' and 'misery' of human beings." Dignity and misery not only in physical terms, though those, but also in the deepest spiritual terms, full or pinched life terms.

I'm coming to be persuaded by Niebuhr's point. Not "only" from the standpoint of the Christ-revelation, but at least from that standpoint "is it possible to look at the human situation without illusion and without despair." At least from that standpoint because I am also persuaded by what Reinhold's brother, H. Richard Niebuhr, said: "Jesus is the unique but not exclusive revelation of God."

The simplicity of the gospel is that somehow God was there in what the Babe of Bethlehem grew up to be and do. One of Queen Elizabeth's advisors back in the sixteenth century told her, "People must be able to touch the Divine here on earth. They must have something higher than themselves to worship." The mystery is that in Jesus, the human one, the divine comes close enough for us to touch, and yet stays higher than ourselves.

But we are reluctant to engage Jesus. We seem to prefer a more abstract, removed God. We prefer the old rules, our rules, rather than the new rules of engagement God gives in Christ, new rules that break those of our little goods and lesser gods, our defensive claims of innocence, our rules of logic, our elevation of profit motives and power struggles, our argument that greed is a virtue and consumption the ultimate freedom, our fascination with violence, our retreat from community, our frantic denial of death. Maybe we prefer to be afraid.

"Only in the 'simplicity of the gospel' is it possible to measure the full 'dignity' and 'misery' of human beings."

Our full dignity is a wondrous thing—the music, the beauty we create, the love, the labor to be just, the gifts of healing, our reach toward peace. But for me, it is our misery that wakes me sweating in the night. Misery not so much of poverty, except of spirit, but the misery of fear. It is hard not to be afraid, and I cannot manage that on my own, or even with others for more than a moment. Fear of my frailty, my taintedness, my limitations, my betrayals and failures, my mortality, my death. I think the fear is part, maybe the core, of my sins. The sins Jesus will save me from. So says Joseph's angel, his dream. And my dream and your dream, too. I only wish that saving didn't take so long.

It begins with Annie Dillard's realizing that when Christ washed his disciples' feet, it was as if he were saying it is all right—believe it or not—to be people, to be human beings, because he became one, too. So, it's okay to be afraid. At least a little. Most of us want, and try, to be in control of the chaos and uncertainty of our lives. We don't like uncertainty. We are afraid of it. And yet, down deep, we know we don't control, and can't control, the uncertainties and contingencies of our lives.

So what's the point? The point is that Christmas, that Jesus, isn't meant to help our "reason" find answers. Jesus is meant to *disarm* our reason. Uncertainty, terrible things, death will keep happening. But it's all right to be human beings. Our fear tears us open, makes us aware of how vulnerable and needy we are all the way down inside. What wakes us sweating in the night, what sends shivers down our spines, cramps our stomachs and loosens our bowels, is exactly where God comes close and touches us—in the smelly dirty manger; in the hard-scrabble roads, shoulder-rubbing with the needy and the powerful; in the shadowy, sweaty struggles in the midnight of our decisions; and, finally, in our deaths.

These are the new rules of engagement to topple the old ones, topple the claims we make for our goodness and our innocence and our smarts, topple our insistence that we deserve what we want but know we can't get on our own or by our rules. Then there is grace, and it's what we want most deeply in life, and it's a gift. So, in the darkness of our fear, we are invited to turn toward the light. We're invited to stumble our way to the manger. We're invited to risk kneeling, risk praying, risk sinning on boldly, risk trusting that Jesus will, and even now is, saving us from our sins by turning our fear of death in all its insidious little and large forms into the way to life.

It happens through the new rules of engagement with Christ, and so with ourselves and with all our brothers and sisters. It's God's grace all the way through. And so, says Dillard, and Joseph, and Jesus, it's all right, even a great gift, to be people, and we can go our way "exultant, in a daze, dancing, to the twin silver trumpets of praise."[8]

Amen.

~

1.   I am greatly indebted to Barbara Krasner, Ph.D., and a collaborator in the formation of Contextual Family Therapy for the provocative distinction between connection and engagement. However, she is not accountable for the interpretation and application of that distinction relative to "New Rules of Engagement."

2.   Ntozake Shange, *for colored girls who have considered suicide when the rainbow is enuf* (New York: Scribner, 1975), 38-39.

3.   Oriah Mountain Dreamer, "The Invitation," *The Invitation* (San Francisco: HarperSanFrancisco, 1999), 1-2.

4.   I am indebted to my colleague Ann Marie Donohue, Ph.D., for her many insights concerning *Saving Private Ryan*. Our discussions are reflected in this interpretation of the film.

5.   Oriah Mountain Dreamer, "The Invitation."

6.   Annie Dillard, *Teaching A Stone To Talk: Expeditions and Encounters* (New York: Harper & Row, 1982), 20.

7.   Abraham Lincoln, Second Inaugural Address, March 4, 1865.

8.   Annie Dillard, *Pilgrim at Tinker Creek* (New York: Harper & Row, 1974), 271.

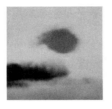

Catch-153

John 21

It's Easter again, with all its pageantry and proclamations. Anthems trumpet, lilies trumpet back, and alleluias echo everywhere. Yet under it all, our eternal longing still collides with our earthy limitations, and our ambivalence lingers despite the excitement of the day. For the most part, we know more of the loss and slow leak of sadness than we do of bliss. Dare we be honest, we might admit there's an undertow of skepticism in the tide of hope that brings us to this day.

Maybe to catch the resurrection we have to glance off to the side of it. The best place to look might not be at the angels, or empty tomb or upper room, but at a stinking fishing boat bobbing out there on the sea of Tiberius with waves slapping against its side and weariness settling in on its occupants. Whatever day was about to dawn at that moment, it wasn't the Sabbath or they wouldn't have been out there fishing. That's one of the things to see, looking off to the side: The resurrection didn't happen on an appointed religious day.

It happened on what would be the equivalent of our Monday, that groan-and-gripe day when, like it or not, you haul yourself out of bed, hitch up your belt, and hike yourself off again to the chaotic thick, or the boring thin, of whatever the routine is for you. Who would ever think to keep an eye out for a resurrection on that kind of a day? But that is just when it happens, if the stories tell it at all straight. And that's enough to fasten our attention on this fishing boat for a moment. It's our kind of scene, our kind of people. So we lean forward a little and squint to get a better look at them, off to the side there in that muffled place between sea and sky, darkness and dawn.

And there they are, Peter and his partners, in their creaking old boat at the end of a not-so-good night of fishing when the empty tomb seems a lot less relevant to them than their empty hold. Isn't that the way it goes? We fish for whatever it is—perks, promotions, or popularity—to prove whatever it is we feel we have to prove—our worth, our importance, or our loveableness. And, as all that gets measured, the bottom line is brutally clear: no fish, no worth. In there somewhere, perhaps, is a vague, fleeting intimation of human limits which hint of death, that familiar, gut-wrenching experience of a slow leak in expectations that has so many variations: the disciples' empty nets or our flat-line-type let down in a 'Don't call us, we'll call you' response to a best-shot interview.

Fix just that moment in your mind. It's not hard to imagine, is it? Don't you suppose Peter and the others are standing there gripping the side of the boat, griping about their luck, staring into the mist and ugly memories rising off the sea, a mix of sweat and tears, and rain maybe, dripping off their noses, someone spitting out a curse, someone yawning, someone scratching their behind and . . . hey, someone *does* call them!

"Friends!"

Who is that booby yelling at them, stirring them from their stupor?

Maybe that's how resurrections always start, with some voice calling—who knows for sure whose it is, or where it comes from, exactly, only that we hear it. That's all and that's enough! Someone calls: a bird, a kid in the alley, a singer on a car radio, a friend on the phone, a word or two from a stranger across the room or the next table, our own voice maybe. No matter, some voice is always calling us or we wouldn't be here this day—or any place any day, probably—and maybe the voice comes from out there somewhere, or inside somewhere, or both. Who knows anything for sure, except we hear it.

So a voice calls Peter and the others, and sets off a confusion as full of comedy as a blend of Woody Allen and Eddie Murphy—or as funny as we might look if we could see ourselves hustling to get it together after the alarm goes off Monday a.m. and we're about to miss the train and can't find the other shoe, or the keys, or the phone number we're supposed to call that day, and the toilet won't shut off, and there's not enough cash around for a train ticket and . . . then, somehow, there's the voice, "Friends, have you caught anything?"

And you scream, "You gotta be kidding!"

But the voice persists, "Shoot the net to the starboard side and you'll make a catch."

Now wait a minute! What do you mean, try something different. We fish from the port side, the way we learned. That's the way it's supposed to be done. But then what have we got to lose so . . . holy mackerel, or perch or bass or cod or whatever that mess of squirming fish is . . . why didn't we think of the starboard side? Or did we? Whose voice was that anyway?

"It is the Lord!" One of them guessed. Could be, sure. That's who it is! And Peter, bless his bumbling heart, gets so excited (or so embarrassed because he's been fishing in the buff) that he puts his clothes on and jumps overboard to swim to shore, which is stupid and backward, but isn't it the day for it?

. . . "Why won't that toilet stop running, and damn this knotted shoelace, and the toast is burning, and oh yeah, I'll be home late, and . . . hey, answer the phone will ya' and tell the idiot who's calling that I'm not here . . . what does he mean, 'Would I be interested in a free week in Martinique if I invest in a condo there?' And, oh God, I'm going to miss the train . . ."

It is funny, isn't it? Like putting on your clothes in your craziness to get into the swim. So everyone laughs and yells and makes their way to shore as best they can, dragging the fish behind them.

And there they are, off to the side, at precisely another moment to fix in your mind. It's not hard to imagine either, is it? After all, what would you do in those circumstances? Don't you suppose they kept looking at each other sideways, nudging each other like schoolboys, shuffling and stammering as people do when they can't get their hearts or minds around something? It's a stupendous thing that's happening. Jesus is back. Well, do you know what those disciples did right then? They counted the fish. At a time like that, they counted the fish! Ah, but it is just there, off to the side in something that seems ridiculous, that we catch something of what the resurrection is about. Hey, how many fish, or minutes, or chances do we have here? 1, 2, 3 . . .

Jacob Bronowski, that magnificent mathematician/ physicist/poet, gives us a clue. He writes: "When a man counts 'one, two, three,' he is not only doing mathematics; he is on the path to the mysticism of numbers in Pythagoras and Vitruvious and Kepler, to the Trinity and the signs of the Zodiac . . . and before we know how it happened . . . the numbers have conspired to make a match with nature."[1]

Ah yes: 1, 2, 3 . . . the mysticism of numbers, the Trinity and strange signs; 28, 29, 30 . . . before we know how it happens, a match with nature and with grace; 41, 42, 43 . . . tulips, and pussy willows, and rain filling the rivers and stirring the seeds; 103, 104, 105 . . . the mystery and the miracle of everything, such as us opening our eyes in the morning, and a couple making love, and a child making sense of markings on a page; 133, 134, 135 . . . a choir singing *"Dona nobis pacem"* and the heart indeed feeling peace in the hearing of it, and reading a wondrous story on an old woman's face or in the grope of a baby's fingers; 151, 152, 153 . . .

One hundred and fifty-three fish! One and five and three add up to nine, and numbers that add up to nine are divisible by nine, and if you don't get the point, don't worry. Maybe there isn't one, except for the fun of it. But if we can't laugh at it, maybe we ought to feel a little uneasy because we may be missing the larger point, which is that probably the numbers themselves—and surely the nature they conspire to make a match with—are gifts, pure gifts. No matter how eager we are for spring, every year we learn again that it comes by its own numbers, in its own way and time, and therefore, as always, it comes as a gift. So numbers and nature. So life, so the dawn, so the neighbor, so the beloved, so the earth itself—gifts! One hundred and fifty-three fish and a resurrection!

Surely everyone knows Joseph Heller's *Catch-22*. The term has become part of our language. Yossarian is a World War II bomber pilot who wants to be grounded because the other side keeps trying to kill him when he flies over with his bombs. He tries to get a doctor to ground him on the basis that he is crazy, but the doctor tells him he is wasting his time. When Yossarian persists—"Can't you ground someone who is crazy"—the doctor admits that he can. In fact, the rule states that he *has* to ground anyone who is crazy, but the person has to *ask*. Yossarian presses, "So then you can ground me?" To his puzzlement, the doctor says no. "You mean there's a catch?" questions Yossarian. "Sure there's a catch!" answers the doctor. "Catch-22. Anyone who wants to get out of combat duty isn't really crazy."[2]

So Catch-22, which symbolizes everything that says you can't win, not really, not finally. Most of us, most of the time, live by catch-22: You can't win.

Then comes Easter, and another catch, God's catch, Catch-153, which says you can't lose, not really, not finally.

Catch-22: You can't win. Catch-153: You can't lose. Scholars who dabble in the mysticism of numbers suggest that the number 153 represents all the varieties of fish in the world, which is to say, all the varieties of people in the world, all caught and held in the net of God's grace. So another thing to see off the side in the story is that, no matter what, the net holds it all. Whatever the load, the net doesn't break. There's a place in the kingdom for all us poor fish.

So, 149, 150, 151 . . . can't you hear the laughter building in their bellies and spilling out of their throats as they count . . . 152, 153—Catch-153—and who would have believed it possible? I think whoever said that only when we hear the gospel as God's wild joke do we hear it at all, was definitely on to something. So here is the gospel cast in miniature: the disciples counting their fish, and we running to catch the train and breathlessly discovering it's even later than we are, and everyone joining in the laughter of God's joke in saving all kinds of fish in God's kingdom—carp and minnows and suckers, blues and bullheads, eels and whales, and all the rest, whatever kind we are, even whatever kind we don't like.

Suddenly in the laughter of it, we begin to wonder if maybe all those impossible things Jesus talked about aren't impossible after all: camels squeezing through the eye of a needle; mountains getting up and moving; mustard seeds growing into row houses for birds; the blind given sight, the deaf their hearing; the vested powers shaken; someone dressing up in something like a tuxedo or evening gown, tapping on the shoulders of drunks and idiots and prostitutes and us—and our enemies—inviting us all to a great champagne and candlelight party. Someone going a second mile with us, and a third, and a fourth—or is it us with them? Or both? And Catch-153, we can't lose, not really. We don't have to fish anymore to prove anything. Life is a gift, pure and simple, and there's no end to it, no end!

But there is a beginning to it, or can be. That's really what Easter is about, and maybe that's what the disciples finally got through their thick skulls, or their heavy hearts, out there on the beach. Resurrection isn't just about life without end, but it's about life that begins, now, eternally now. John Donne, that poet-priest, put the point to verse in "Hymn To My God, in My Sickness":

> Since I am coming to that holy room,
> where, with thy choir of saints for evermore
> I shall be made thy music, as I come
> I tune the instrument here at the door,
> and what I may do then, think here before.[3]

Yes, think here before, and sing, blow, play here before, which is to say risk living now! Catch-153, and there's the risen Lord on the beach, setting those disciples to music, and if it sounds like laughter, it means they got the point at last. Life without end can begin!

So they begin by moving on to something very simple. They had breakfast together, and that is another off-to-the-side moment to fix in your mind. A small fire, some bread and fish, the smell of the sea, gulls screaming hello to the morning, a few friends, and something between them, and in them, something we can't really define except love is the best name we have for it—and remember, it is love that never ends, love that nothing can separate us from.

And there it is: breakfast and love!

An old friend, Edward Huber, felt that haunt of grace and responded to it for us all in something he wrote on a holiday greeting card he sent years ago: "We look across the table for the thousandth time at the children, the friends, the beloved. Is [God] so close after all, leading us again and again from dark valleys to the ecstasy of the familiar? The One we have longed for is already among us."

That haunt is a key to resurrection, to eternal life beginning: the ecstasy of the familiar, being simple, staying simple, and staying watchful, lest we miss the resurrections of the daily. Staying simple and watchful means letting go, doesn't it? Letting go of many things, letting go of ourselves, maybe! It is, after all—*before* all—God's day, and all of it is a gift: life and everything about it. Maybe whatever is coming unraveled for us—marriage, job, life itself—maybe whatever it is can't begin again until we do let go, a little. Letting go: the disciples of their familiar fishing boat, launching off into a suddenly strange and wondrous world, and we of whatever familiar, stifling thing it is we hang on to so tightly—a grudge, a resentment, a guilt, a lie we're living, a borderline rage, a certainty of our rightness that is choking us, and everyone else, to death.

Do you remember that delightful scene in *The Belle of Amherst* where Emily Dickinson reads the newspaper to her sister Vinnie one evening? It goes like this: Emily says, "Oh here's one you'll love Vinnie. 'TRAIN HITS WOMAN ON MILL RIVER TRESTLE.' 'Cornelia Snell, fifty-four . . . was killed last Wednesday by the Belchertown express as she struggled vainly to free her foot from a railroad switch.' Her foot, Vinnie! 'Engineer Grover W. Putnam declared, "By the time I saw the poor lady and her dog, it was too late." . . . Oh, the dog survived! It jumped clear! . . . Her children are planting an evergreen in her memory near the spot. Isn't that sweet, Vinnie?" Then after a long pause, Emily says in simple wonder, "I wonder why she didn't take off her shoe?"[4]

The question is the same for each of us: What do we need to take off, let go of, if we are going to live—or begin to? Catch-153 says we can't lose, so let go. We don't have to fish anymore to prove anything. We can tune our instrument for the joy of it, our instrument, our authentic self, and here at the door of eternity, begin to play the music of what we know as love wherever we experience it or sense the need for it, and so begin to live it out with all the courage and imagination and joy we can muster.

Live it out! That, too, is what Easter is about: beginning to live it out. And that is what the struggle for justice is about: love with its sleeves rolled up, love with bloody feet and wounded hands and a won't-quit glint in its eye. Love with its sleeves rolled up and laughter on its lips. And it means no one is left in tombs: not the poor whose children go hungry and have no medical insurance, or African Americans in urban ghettos, or gays, or women, or children, or Arabs, or Jews, or Palestinians, or Third World people, or old people, no one! Justice means no one is left in bad schools, or in unending wars of revenge, or polluted water, or ozone layers with holes punched in it, or acid rain. Justice and peace, human community, is love lived out.

So the disciples, there on the beach—and us wherever we are—are called to a deep kind of sharing, or the beginning of it. That also involves a profound kind of letting go. To see it, you have to look off to the side, and then off to the side again, and then fix in your mind one last moment. There is Jesus telling Peter three times to feed his sheep, which is quite a lofty calling, if you look at it one way, which Peter did, being Peter—and being like us.

"Feed my sheep." Care for the world and all my children. So question one: "Why me?" And if me, then surely there's a pay-off for that kind of commission. So question two: "For what?" Those were Peter's questions, and now they're ours.

But keep looking at Peter standing there—wrestling with himself and the feel of it, flexing his shoulders as if the weight of that way of looking at it were already chafing a bit (as we know it does), and so, scratching his ear, drubbing his nose, rumpling his hair, and sorting out the questions he couldn't quite put a handle of words on.

Then out of the corner of his eye, he spots another disciple, someone he loves, and somehow it all comes clear to him. He points to the other disciple and says, "Lord, what about him?" It's not very hard to imagine that moment and that question, is it? It's not really such a bad question, either. If we listen carefully, we'll find as much concern for the other person in it as a cop-out for Peter. After all, being like Peter, we wonder, too, "How can I care about people without controlling them and the outcome of what I want for them—and the world? How can I love without feeling I need to manage things according to how and why and where I love? How can I feed without investing myself in those I feed and wanting a return on my investment?

"Lord, what about him?" What about my father, my mother, my brother or sister, my husband or wife, my son or daughter, my friend, my colleague, my neighbor, my enemy? If I do things for them, don't they owe me? Shouldn't they do what I know is right for them? What about their struggles, their success, their life, their death? What's the reward for my being so involved and vulnerable?

Not a bad question! It comes close to the heart of this day. *"Lord, what about him, her, them?"*

Cock your head off to the side now, and listen to Jesus' answer over the pounding of the surf and the timpani of your heart: *"If it is my will that he remain until I come, what is that to you?"* With that, we get reminded again of what we keep forgetting about this Easter day: It isn't *our* day at all, except as a gift. It is really God's day. Ultimately God is in charge of it and every day, and of what happens in them, or to us, or to anyone. That's the awesome, amazing freedom of the resurrection. *"If it is my will . . ."* Which is to say, the mystery of it is past finding out. It's all a gift, all grace. Catch-153! Tune your instrument for the joy of it, not the applause or the reward.

I've watched the video of *The Wizard of Oz* many times with my grandchildren. They think it's scary until almost the end. And many of the encounters Dorothy and the Lion and the Scarecrow and the Tin Man have along the Yellow Brick Road—with the growling wicked witches, their foreboding castle, the Haunted Forest, and the screeching winged monkeys—are pretty hair-raising. Then they finally get to the wizard who they're sure will grant their wishes. They plead their case to the wizard who is hidden behind a screen, but all they get are smoke belches and a loud, booming voice. Then, in a scuffle the screen gets knocked over, and the wizard gets exposed as only a little bald-headed man whose power is all smoke and mirrors.

In frustration Dorothy screams at him, "You are a very bad man!"

The little man replies, "Oh no, my dear. I'm really a very good man, but I'm a very bad wizard." My grandchildren always laugh and clap at that. I join them because in that moment our fears get knocked down a peg or two.

Even so, Jesus' resurrection knocks over our screen and exposes us to ourselves, if we look off to the side. The truth is that we are bad wizards, bad gods, but good human beings—or *pretty good* ones. More importantly, we are *loved* human beings. That's the secret, and it's a saving and liberating one. We don't need to pretend to be wizards, or angels, anymore. Life with the feel of eternity about it is not anything we can give to anyone, including ourselves. But it is a gift that comes anyway, and keeps coming. It is something to accept, to point to, to share, to rejoice in, and that's the wonder.

So the liberating mystery is that we can only begin living as very good human beings when we accept that we are very bad wizards, even worse gods. But never mind. Today—every day—is a gift still and all to us very human beings. This day, all days, this life, life forever and the living of it.

"If it is my will . . . what is that to you?" Which is to say that nothing happens God can't handle, even with wounded hands. We can let go of ourselves, our lies and illusions and pretenses. We can dare to love just for the joy of it, love because deeper than anything else, we're lovers, and not to love is to deny our lives. We can let go of those we've loved who have died, for they are in God's hands. In the letting go, there's something of peace and healing. We can even let go of enemies. We can love them because they're just "human merely beings," as e. e. cummings puts it, as are we. And not to see that is to miss a resurrection or 2, or 3, or 4 . . . let go and forgive and feed sisters and brothers the world around in the freedom of it; 10, 11, 12 . . . share with them for the joy of it; 77, 78, 79 . . . bad wizards but good humans beings, matched with a kingdom . . . 97, 98, 99 . . .

And the matching goes a little like this scene from Herbert Tarr's *The Conversion of Chaplain Cohen.* David, the adopted boy now grown, is leaving home. He stands on a railroad platform saying good-bye to the adoptive parents he calls uncle and aunt. He takes their rough hands in his. "How can I ever begin to repay you two for what you've done for me!"

Uncle Asher speaks gently, "David, there's a saying: 'The love of parents goes to their children but the love of these children goes to their children.' "

David protests, "That's not so. I'll always be trying to . . . "

Aunt Devorah interrupts him: "David, what your Uncle Asher means is that a parent's love isn't to be paid back; it can only be passed on."[5]

There it is!

141, 142, 143 . . . God the Father and the Mother of us all, and Easter and the Risen Lord and something there is just no name for but love, and joy; 148, 149, 150 . . . something we can't repay, but only pass on the best way we can; 151, 152, 153. Catch-153, and no matter leaky toilets and missed trains and aching problems and all the thick and thin of it, we can't lose. But we can begin the passing on of love and the living that doesn't end. Alleluia.

~

1.   Jacob Bronowski, *A Sense of the Future* (Cambridge, MA: The MIT Press, 1977), 29,31.

2.   Joseph Heller, *Catch-22: A Dramatization* (New York: Delta Publishing Co., Inc., 1971), 11-13.

3.   John Donne, *The Complete English Poems* (Baltimore, MD: Penguin Education 1971), 347.

4.   William Luce, *The Belle of Amherst: A Play Based on the Life of Emily Dickinson* (Boston: Houghton Mifflin Company, 1976), 32-33.

5.   Herbert Tarr, *The Conversion of Chaplain Cohen* (New York: Avon Books, A Division of The Hearst Corp, 1963), 32.

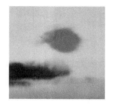

The Song
of the Disordered One

Mark 1:14-20

During a telephone conversation, my friend Bill Coffin commented that a lot of people hold certainty dearer than truth. Many seem to hold to the British academic's allegiance to the position that "Nothing should ever be done for the first time."

That shoe fits most of us. We much prefer certainty to uncertainty because uncertainty is one of our greatest fears. So we try to hold it off by holding fast to our habits, biases, and opinions. The sad consequence is that insisting on certainty means forfeiting creativity. That distorts the gospel and shrinks our lives.

It's unimaginable how dull and deprived our world would be without the creativity of composers, artists, poets, writers, performers across the ages. We rightly rejoice over the gifts of those creative giants. But surely it is misguided to limit the notion of creativity to them. Creativity includes the art of life itself. It's about the way we live and work, what we risk, and why.

It's about Jesus calling Peter and Andrew and James and John to follow him. What's so stunning is that, without any negotiation about wages, benefits, and pension plans, these four drop their fish nets and take off after him. That seems unbelievable, even irresponsible. How could they do such a thing? They had obligations to meet, bills to pay. Why would they do such a chancey thing? It goes against our grain. It's too romantic. It makes no sense.

Or does it? Just on the face of it, what Peter and Andrew and James and John did suggests that much of what we assume is fixed, irrefutable, unchangeable, really isn't. Maybe Peter and his buddies had hit the ditch of their unlived lives and believed they were stuck there. Some of us might know what that's like. But Jesus flings open something different for them, and us. He insists that life can change, we can change. That's what creativity is about. That's what the gospel is about. And it's both appealing and scary. What does it mean?

Recently I came across the definition of a leader as being a non-anxious presence. Don't you suppose that's what Jesus was for the disciples, and why they followed him? Even so, that's what Jesus is for us, too: a non-anxious presence. He takes the fear—or enough of it—out of uncertainty to energize creativity. To live creatively does take faith, faith in a non-anxious presence who shows there is more to the world, to life, to us, than can be contained in all our little certainties.

There are possibilities yet untapped in us. There are dimensions yet unexplored around us. There are chances yet to be taken on the way to becoming free, to making love, to doing justly, to shaping beauty, to going deeper into the mysteries of God's kingdom. Christ calls us to be about that creativity. Come, follow me.

David Ogston, a minister in Perth, Scotland, recently sent me a letter about some things I'd written. In his letter he said, "Here's my thank you. It comes from the pen of Iain Crichton Smith, one of our poets (Scotland is awash with poets)":

Children, follow the dwarfs and the giants and the wolves,
into the Wood of Unknowing, into the leaves

where the terrible granny perches and sings to herself
past the tumultuous seasons high on her shelf . . .

Avoid the Man with the Book, the Speech Machine,
and the Rinsoed Boy who is forever clean.

Keep clear of the Scholar and the domestic Dog
and, rather than the Sunny Smoothness, choose the Fog.

Follow your love, the butterfly, where it spins
over the wall, the hedge, the road, the fence,

and love the Disordered Man who sings like a river
whose form is Love, whose country is Forever.[1]

I read that as a powerful description of Jesus: *"the Disordered Man who sings like a river whose form is Love, whose country is Forever."*

So, what is the song this Disordered One sings to us?

The first stanza is that certainty is not all it's cracked up to be. A little girl riding home from church asked her father, "Daddy, why does the Bible always say, 'And it came to pass,' and never says, 'It came to stay'?"

Well, how would you answer? The reason is because nothing ever comes to stay. Change is inevitable. Think of all we thought was certain before September 11, 2001. Now all that certainty has tumbled with the towers. We've experienced how limited, vulnerable, fragile, and yet imaginative and talented we are. Change comes, swiftly or gradually, but it comes because it's part of God's creation. It makes creativity not only possible but necessary.

The question isn't whether there will be change, but whether we will bend it to the good in our personal life and in our life together. Out of the chances in uncertainty, can we, will we, make our lives and our world more humane, more just, more fair and lovely?

You've probably heard the story of the old man in Ireland who lived alone. His only son was in prison as a political enemy of the government, and the old man didn't know who would spade up his potato garden for planting. So he wrote his son about his problem. From prison his son wrote back, "For heaven's sake, don't dig up that garden. That's where I buried the guns!"

Early one morning a couple of days after the old man got his son's letter, a dozen British soldiers invaded the garden and dug the whole thing up but didn't find any guns. The old man was bewildered and wrote to his son telling him what happened and asking him what to do next. The son's answer was, "Just plant your potatoes."

Now that's creativity in action. It helps shape the world—in spades. Don't you imagine that kind of ingenious creativity would make any entrenched power tremble a little? It's about the creativity of the common life. What revolution is waiting for us to take a risk in our life, at our work, in our neighborhood? What word can we speak, what deed can we do, what resistance can we make, what options can we offer that might create something new for us and for others?

We know the familiar story of that ragged band of Israelites coming to the Red Sea with Pharaoh's army in hot pursuit. But as someone pointed out, the real miracle of the exodus wasn't so much the parting of the Red Sea at that moment as it was the first few Israelites daring to step out into the mud and begin crossing to the other side. They, like Moses, were a non-anxious presence encouraging the panicky fugitives to follow. And they did!

Creativity takes audacity. What we say is certain, isn't. What we assume is fixed and inviolable doesn't have to be that way. John Updike suggests that what we admire most about Jesus is his audacity. It was audacity that changed water to wine, that gave sight to the blind, that challenged the established powers with another vision of what God's kingdom was about. Listen to the song of the Disordered One whose country is forever, and follow, risk, create something new in your life, for the life of others.

~

What is the song the Disordered One sings to us?

The second stanza is that things are not always what they seem. Antoine de Saint Exupéry, who wrote that wonderful book *The Little Prince*, said, "It is only with the heart that one can see rightly; what is essential is invisible to the eye."[2]

Among other things, I take that to mean that it's when we see that something different might be possible, it becomes possible. So half of creativity is seeing possibilities. That kind of seeing is what I mean by imagination. I keep saying that imagination is the dancing partner of faith. We're conditioned into thinking science gives the only true view of the world, that what's real can be measure, weighed, replicated. But is that so? Is what is real about you, or me, what can be measured? No, life is too dynamic for that.

In a little book entitled *The Meaning of It All*, the great Nobel Laureate physicist Richard Feynman writes about how critical uncertainty is to creativity in science: "Nothing is certain or proved beyond all doubt. You investigate for curiosity, because it is *unknown*, not because you know the answer."[3]

That touches on the mystery of God and the freedom faith gives us. Feynman goes helpfully on: "It is a great adventure to contemplate the universe beyond [humanity] . . . When . . . the mystery and majesty of matter are fully appreciated, to then turn

the objective eye back on [humans] as matter, to see life as part
of the universal mystery of greatest depth . . . usually ends in
laughter and a delight in the futility of trying to understand.
These scientific views end in awe and mystery, lost at the edge in
uncertainty . . ."[4] Feynman goes even deeper when he describes
himself, and us, as he stands at the edge of the sea: ". . . living
things, masses of atoms. DNA, protein . . . dancing a pattern
ever more intricate . . . out of the cradle onto the dry land . . .
here it is standing . . . atoms with consciousness . . . matter with
curiosity . . . wonders at wondering . . ."[5]

You don't have to get that exactly to grasp that Feynman is
saying is that life is shot through with mystery, with possibilities,
and so with wonder. Those are the ingredients of wonder, and
creativity begins and continues in wonder. In a hundred ways Jesus shows that God puts us at the edge of uncertainty because
that's where we are propelled toward the kingdom if we are dar-
ingly faithful.

*"Love the Disordered Man who sings like a river . . . whose country
is Forever."*

Jesus is the non-anxious presence bidding us to see ourselves and the world differently, and so to live creatively.

Seeing differently. In an article about authors who offer a
"whisper of hope," Doris Betts says, "Cormac McCarthy writes
about a blind amputee who is arguing with a street preacher.
The beggar says, 'Look at me, legless and everything. I reckon
you think I ought to love God.' The preacher answers, 'Yeah, I
reckon you ought. An old blind mess and a legless fool is a flower
in the garden of God.' "[6]

That hints at the creativity of seeing. Of looking past the
surface and seeing people, whoever they are, whoever you are,
however wounded, messed up, difficult, as flowers in the garden
of God. Of looking beneath appearances to see that things and
people are not always what they seem. Of reaching out to others

with compassion, with mercy, joining in a mutual nudge toward justice. No big thing . . . or is it? What does it mean to love our neighbor and our enemies as ourselves? Goethe said that once we see and make a commitment, the whole universe moves. Maybe that's too grandiose, but something moves, even a little, and that's a major beginning. That's what creativity dares in the dance with uncertainty.

That's how the song of the Disordered One urges us to live: To follow our love over the walls of fear and narrow nationalism, over the hedges of racism and religious dogmatism, over the fences of poverty and exploitation. To shape uncertainty into justice and peace and beauty and a glad inclusion of everyone into the feast of the human family. It invites us on toward the country of forever.

~

What is the song the Disordered One sings to us?

The third stanza is, finally, this: Time is not always as confined or as small as it seems. There's a story of two old friends, Ed and Max, who live in the same neighborhood. Every morning, Ed appears at the door of Max's house and Max is ready. Then they go for a walk together. One morning, Ed turns to Max and asks, "What is your name again?" The two friends walk on a few steps, and Max turns to Ed and says, "How soon do you have to know?"

That's not quite so funny when you're older and stick it on the calendar of your own life, or when you're young and live on the anxious edge of urgency. Most of us, most of the time, want to know the answers and the outcome of things today, or at worst, tomorrow. It's part of our compulsion to have certainty, and it stifles creativity because creativity takes time.

So it takes patience, and for me at least, patience is in short supply. And so, therefore, is creativity. I give up much too soon. I get discouraged much too soon. I become pessimistic much too quickly. Do you?

But healing, justice, peace, reconciliation—all the things creativity is about in the artistry of our little lives and our small world—take time. How much time? Perhaps more time than any one of us has. But they will not take more time than God has. It is good to remember, as often as we can, that there is a non-anxious presence with us all the time, wherever we are.

"Love the Disordered One who sings like a river . . . whose country is Forever."

Forever is what we are part of, what our little creativity stretches out toward. That's why, more than anyone else, people of faith don't have to be afraid to fail. We need fear only not risking, not daring to be creative. Outcomes are up to God, and so are resurrections—of us, and of our failed efforts.

I go back to a story I love about buzzards because it's true, it's funny, and at heart it's about creativity and time. The buzzards are the ones who were supposed to be in a scene in the movie *Hud*. You may remember the story. In the movie, set and filmed in Texas, Paul Newman was supposed to ride up, discover a dead cow, look up at a tree branch lined with buzzards, and in his distress over the loss of the cow, fire his gun at one of the buzzards. Then all the other buzzards were supposed to fly into the wild blue.

Well, the first problem with shooting the scene was the scruffy condition of the local buzzards. So more photogenic buzzards had to be flown in at considerable expense. The second problem, more formidable, was how to keep the buzzards sitting on the tree branch until it was time for them to fly. The solution was to wire their feet to the branch, and then when Newman fires his gun, to pull the wire, release their feet and allow them to take off.

But the film makers had not reckoned with the mentality of buzzards. With their feet wired, the buzzards had balance problems but enough mobility to pitch forward. When they tried to fly, they hung upside down from the branch with their wings flopping. Not a good outcome for dramatic effect. Plus the circulatory system of buzzards doesn't work upside down. So after a minute or two, they passed out, hanging limp from the tree branch. That wasn't what Hollywood had in mind.

After six or seven episodes of pitching forward, passing out, being revived, being put back on the branch, pitching forward again, the buzzards gave up. So when the wire was pulled the next time and their feet released, they sat there, saying in their nonverbal sneer, "We tried that before. It did not work. We are not going to try it again." So they had to bring in a high-powered buzzard therapist to restore their self-esteem.[7]

I suppose we could go in a lot of different directions applying that story to the topic of creativity, including the forward flop. But the point I have in mind, and heart, comes out of my own experience, and out of the gospel. Most of us have had the equivalent experience of the buzzard flop, and like them, have given up and settled into a less risky, less humiliating life style. But we aren't buzzards, and that life style, though safe, isn't too joyful.

The gospel says take the risks no matter how many times you flop. Take the risks as many times as there are risks to take to imagine yourself whole and loving and a blessing, to mend a breech between you and someone, to do something for the sake of justice, to say your truth at whatever cost, to exercise compassion, to create something beautiful, to lift someone left by the side of the road, or the pew, or your desk or house.

∼

What is the song the Disordered One sings to us?

The song is not complete with only three stanzas. There are blanks for you to fill in. That's so because it's an invitation to be creative, and no one can be creative for you.

As you sing your particular verse, remember that a non-anxious presence is with you always, to the end of the earth. That's reason to rejoice for the creativity you can live.

Follow your love, the butterfly, where it spins
over the wall, the hedge, the road, the fence,

and love the Disordered Man who sings like a river
whose form is Love, whose country is Forever.

∼

1. "Children, Follow the Dwarfs" by Iain Crichton Smith, *Collected Poems* (Manchester, UK: Carcanet, 1992).

2. Antoine de Saint Exupéry, *The Little Prince* (New York: Harcourt, Brace & World, Inc., 1943), 87.

3. Richard P. Feynman, *The Pleasure of Finding Things Out* (Cambridge, MA: Helix Books Perseus Publishing, 1999), 248.

4. Ibid., 250.

5. Ibid., 144.

6. Doris Betts, "Everything I Know About Writing I Learned in Sunday School," *The Christian Century*, October 21, 1998: 966-67.

7. The buzzard story is adapted from "Dancing with Professors: The Trouble with Academic Prose," *The New York Times Book Review*, October 31, 1993: 24.

A Long View
from the Parking Lot

Luke 12:22-34
Philippians 4:4-9

Maybe Jesus had pretty much worn them out by then—those twelve he'd rounded up from fishing boats and tax offices and rebel camps and anywhere else he could find them. Worn them out traipsing all over the country, day and after day, heading out early every morning, even after Jesus had been out praying most of the night. Worn them out with all that shake-things-up preaching and teaching. Worn them out with all that healing of peoples' stomach-turning diseases. Worn them out with all that shoulder rubbing with the smelly poor and hanging out with disreputable sinners, all that befriending of nobody women, and all that stressful bearding the authority lions in their dens. Worn them out until they weren't sure anymore which town they'd left or which one they were going toward.

Worn them out until they began to wonder out loud where the whole thing was headed and what was to become of them. Lately, Jesus had even started talking about death, his own death, and that's certainly a topic to put a kink in a campaign. They'd started out thinking he was the Messiah come to change things, a surefire winner they'd risk backing. But now they'd begun to doubt that he was a viable candidate after all, or one that would last long. As far as they could see, they were in a road show to big trouble. They were worn out, a little fed up, and a lot scared.

So right there, on the dusty road midway between their dreams and their distress, Jesus sits the disciples down and speaks some of the gentlest, most assuring words he ever spoke: "Do not worry about your life . . . for life is more than food, and the body more than clothing." The words resonate. Jesus might well be speaking to us, on the road from there to here to wherever, midway between our weariness and our worries.

And yet, the words are so easily forgotten that we need to hear them again: "Consider the ravens . . ." Not particularly pretty birds or lovely singers, their only sound a grating *kraaak.*

". . . And yet God feeds them. Of how much more value are you than the birds! And can any of you by worrying add a single hour to your span of life? If then you are not able to do so small a thing as that, why do you worry about the rest?"

The words pour out of him—and over us—as haunting as flute music or a Gregorian chant: "Consider the lilies . . . even Solomon in all his glory was not clothed like one of these. But if God so clothes the grass of the field . . . how much more will he clothe you—you of little faith! . . . do not keep worrying . . . Instead, strive for [God's] kingdom, and these things will be given to you as well. Do not be afraid . . . for it is your Father's good pleasure to give you the kingdom. Sell your possessions and give alms . . ."

Those last words—about selling our stuff and giving alms—are less about duty than about freedom. They're about the freedom to take chances and laugh, even in the face of adversity or failure, or death itself. We don't have to pinch, or grasp, or crouch, or run. But even if we do, the words haunt us, stir our longing: *Do not worry. Do not be afraid.* Why? Because God is at work in it all.

My friend Rick Josiassen recently included in a note to me some words of Yale professor of philosophy Dr. Eugene Rosenstock-Huessy. The words touch on the meaning of what Jesus is saying: "If we take the short view, we can make God a liar. But if we take the long view, we can see the glorious, unfolding mystery."[1] Look at things in the short view, and they're a blur. But take the long view, things come into focus. Short term is face-value, long term is grace-value.

Faith is more than half about taking the long view. Don't you suppose that's why Jesus used those nature images in what he spells out to the disciples sitting there by the roadside—and to us sitting wherever we're sitting now? Jesus is emphasizing that more than present appearances are called for in taking the long view. The long view goes beyond the surface of "now" to swim the dimension of depth. God works beneath the surface, beyond the appearances, more attentively than the ticking of time, under, ahead of any given moment. Taking the long view is about paying attention to the slow work of the mysterious, persistent haunt of grace.

So there they are, the disciples, halfway between the fishing boats they left bobbing behind and the splintery cross they are headed for, and Jesus is telling them to focus on the kingdom of God, to take the long view and to not be afraid. *"Consider the ravens . . . Consider the lilies . . ."* At least it is enough to get them on their feet and back on the road.

Surely Jesus words came back to Peter and John like the scent of honeysuckle much later as they stood astonished by the empty tomb that first Easter morning, trying to focus on a view that is longer by an eternity than they'd dared to dream, stretching out past death itself. You see, the gospel is about nothing if it's not about focusing on the long view, on the unfolding mystery of God's grace. Which of us doesn't need the assurance of Jesus' words to see beyond the short term?

So hear them again through a personal experience. It happened on a Sunday morning on the road between the church office and the side entrance to the Education Building. As we all do from time to time, I was feeling worn out, a little fed up, and maybe a lot scared when I drove into the parking lot. About what? About variations on the same things that shrink all of our worlds and shorten our view.

As I got out of the car, wagging my briefcase behind me, I spotted Cakky Braun and her little son, Robert. I called to her, asking if she would wait a minute for me. She stopped where the parking lot meets the ramp into the Education Building.

I studied Cakky as I walked toward her. I swear, she looked like a psychedelic angel with her multicolored scarf wrapped around her head to cover the hair loss from chemotherapy, and her jacket like a field of wild flowers punctuated with rolling mounds that turned out to be pockets bulging with health food snacks.

Recently Cakky had been diagnosed with inflammatory breast cancer, the most aggressive kind. The chemo was to shrink the tumor before surgery. I walked over and asked how she was. She began to give me a long view from the parking lot.

"I've never been better," she said, her eyes glowing like a delighted child's, her words tumbling out with a kind of excitement. "I realize my cancer is truly a chance for me to let God transform my life, and that's happening. People ask me and I tell them there's nothing like a near-catastrophic disease to get you focused on what matters, get your priorities straight. I'm glad that's happening. You know, when the first round of chemo didn't shrink the tumor, I got real down about it. But now I think it was a good thing because if it had worked the first time, it would have been too easy. I had to deal with my fear so I could move ahead."

When I asked her how she did that, she responded, "Diet,

hypnotherapy. But really, the key is I pray all the time. All the time! I don't take God for granted any more. You know?"

I told her I pray for her every day. She gave me a little hug and said, "I know. The prayers of people help. It's the most important thing anyone can do. I pray instead of worry, because if I worry that much, I might as well be dead anyway. Being anxious shrinks your life, you know what I mean?"

I said I absolutely knew that.

She went on, softly "You've really helped me, and I thank you. I know you love me. I'm trying to love everyone. I'm focusing on serving God and being present to my family."

I stood there listening and thinking about what I'd been worried about a few minutes earlier. Whatever it was, it looked pretty puny from where I stood at that moment, at the edge of the parking lot with the long view Cakky was stretching out for me.

"When I got my head together is when things started changing for me." It seemed to me as if Cakky were almost singing somehow. "My tumors are thirty percent smaller than they were. I keep praying. That's what I do now. Every day it's amazing how God gives me quietness and sends kind of deep thoughts, sort of like angels, to keep me going and feeling whole. I'm a lot less afraid now, and fear's really the worst thing about this stuff."

"So you've been healed in the way that matters most," I said, hugging her.

"Yeah, even if I don't get cured," she said. "No matter what happens, I'll be okay. The family will be okay. We've gone through half our savings, but it doesn't matter. If we have to sell the house, we'll be okay. No more worrying about climbing the career ladder, like I was doing before, with my sixty- to seventy-hour weeks. It was crazy. If I have to deliver mail, it'll be fine, being outdoors, getting exercise." Then Cakky added, "Thanks for your love and being there for me. Let me know what I can do for you."

"Pray for me," I said, tearing up.

"I do," she said. "I already do."

"I guess that's why I'm doing as well as I am," I smiled. "But keep praying, will you?"

"Okay. And let me know what else I can do for you, please," she said.

I put my arm around her, and we walked into the building together. I'd been given a great gift, a long view from the parking lot.

"If we take the short view. . ."

If? Mostly we do, don't we?

"But if we take the long view . . ."

What else is the church about except to help each other take the long view? The wonder is that it happens often enough to keep us going.

"Consider the ravens . . . Consider the lilies . . . Strive for God's kingdom . . . Do not be afraid, little flock, for it is your Father-Mother's good pleasure to give you the kingdom."

What does it mean to *strive* for a kingdom if God is *giving* it to us? I used to think, and too much still do, that striving for God's kingdom meant doing all sorts of virtuous things, working for justice, fighting for good causes, making all the effort I could to improve society and the community, efforts that we all willingly and rightly undertake. But maybe too willingly . . . if we get worn out, a little fed up, and maybe a lot scared, blurred by the short view. It's easy to let the long view get out of focus.

Don't misunderstand. I think all our efforts for justice and all our expressions of compassion are good and necessary ways of faith. But I don't think those things are the first thing it means to strive for the kingdom. I think the first way is focusing on the kingdom, focusing on the goodness and grace of God, even in hard times. I think first of all it means taking the long view and seeing "the glorious, unfolding mystery" we are part of *but not responsible for*. We work *out of* God's kingdom, not *for* it. Otherwise, we live joyless, burdened, anxious lives.

I'm coming to grasp—and be grasped by—the wisdom that striving has something to do with what Cakky said: "I pray all the time. All the time! It's amazing how God gives me quietness and sends kind of deep thoughts, sort of like angels, to keep me going and feeling whole. I'm a lot less afraid now, and fear's really the worst thing about this stuff. Shrinks your life, you know what I mean?"

We *do* know, don't we? Striving in faith is about the long view. It's about shrinking our fear a little and expanding our lives a lot. Striving is what Paul wrote about in his letter to the Philippians: "Do not worry about anything, but in everything by prayer and supplication with thanksgiving, let your requests be made known to God. And the peace of God which passes all understanding, will guard your hearts and your minds in Christ Jesus."

The long view is rooted in that peace. Out of that peace, true freedom is born, the freedom not to be afraid. Out of that freedom, our work of compassion and justice is generated. When we pray, with thanksgiving and honesty, our shoulders can drop from up around our ears, and in some deep way, as with Cakky, we can trust—or begin to—that everything will be all right. Otherwise, it just comes down to being worn out, fed up a little, and, sooner or later, scared a lot because no matter how hard we work for good, if the outcome is entirely up to us and our efforts, the game is over.

Keep focused on the long view: "I pray all the time. All the time! . . . I'm a lot less afraid now." What else but the peace of God is that?

I think striving for the kingdom also has to do with daring to be generous. *"Do not be afraid, little flock, for it is your Father-Mother's good pleasure to give you the kingdom. Sell your possessions, and give alms."* That's about freedom, isn't it? That's the long view Cakky was talking about: "No matter what happens, I'll be okay. The family will be okay. We've gone through half our savings, but it doesn't matter. If we have to sell the house, we'll be okay . . . Please tell me what I can do for you."

Whatever else freedom is, it surely involves generosity of spirit. Generosity is a risk. It bets that there really is enough for everyone, so life isn't about grasping and hoarding. Generosity is an antidote for the contagious dis-ease of having more than is good for our souls. Generosity isn't just about giving things and money to good causes and institutions working for justice and peace, though it may mean *at least* that. That kind of generosity can begin a discipline that leads to our freedom of spirit.

But generosity is about more than the giving money. It's about being open to other people, sharing ourselves with them.

"Please tell me what I can do for you," Cakky asked.

"Pray for me," this professional pray-er said from my heart.

"I already do," she said as though she had nothing else to do.

Her generosity carried healing for both of us.

I think generosity is close to the heart of prayer. What if we prayed generously for each other, and for those we think of as enemies? What if we prayed for our leaders and the poor in one breath, for the oppressed and exploited at the same time we prayed for the wealthy struggling with their own kind of oppression? Imagine what answers we might become to our own prayers. Generosity is about giving the precious gift of time to each other. It's paying attention to other people, and that quite literally means paying the cost with a piece of ourselves to attend to others. Generosity stretches us toward the long view.

It's curious how close to science generosity comes. Cakky's experience confirms it. I keep going back to what Nobel Laureate in physics Richard Feynman says about the whole scientific enterprise: It is about the question, "If I do this, what will happen?" and then responding to the question with, "Try it and see."[2] Isn't that essentially what Jesus did? I don't suppose many people thought he could heal people by forgiving them, or give sight to a blind man by mixing clay and spit and smearing it on his eyes, or feeding a crowd of thousands with five loaves and two fish, and so on and on. Most people, including his disciples, would have said out of hand, "If you try that, nothing will happen and you'll have played the fool." But Jesus' spirit was too generous *not* to "try it and see." And lo and behold, look what happened.

Generosity stretches toward the long view. Being peacemakers, going the second mile, loving neighbor and enemy as ourselves, feeding the hungry, caring for the sick, liberating the captives, being merciful, taking the log out of our own eye before dealing with the speck in another's eye. Try it and see.

Will it do any good? Try it and see, and look as far down the road as you can imagine. Try it and see, even with the most unlikely brothers and sisters you can think of, even with your supposed enemies.

Being generous means not giving up our efforts to do justly, or to make peace, or to be trustworthy in our relationships if in the short term, or by the short view, they don't seem to work. Generosity means that risking even the modest gifts and compassionate spirit of each of us not only increases our freedom in grace, but enables God to work slow miracles with us and through us. "Try it and see." Take the long view of yourself.

In the end, maybe something simple is as startling and profound as anything complicated can be. Maybe truth comes in a children's song as powerfully as in the theory of General Relativity or the map of the double helix of the human genetic code. Mostly, we like sophistication because it makes us seem so smart. We can slip away and hide in it, arguing our short-term views which make God a liar, or irrelevant.

But maybe, if we admit it, the straightjacket of sophistication is unbuckled by a simple confession of love that buckles our knees instead, and softens our hearts.

"Do not worry about your life . . . Consider the ravens . . . God feeds them. Of how much more worth are you than the birds . . . Do not be afraid . . . it is your Father's good pleasure to give you the kingdom."

What relief, what peace, what joy, what freedom there would be if we could begin by accepting that gift. I got a glimpse of what it could be when Cakky gave me the gift of a long view from the parking lot. Her honest simplicity cut through all my overblown pretensions of being so smart and sophisticated—or having to be.

Karl Barth was one of the brilliant theologians and biblical scholars of the late twentieth century. Barth wrote many weighty and revolutionary books on a wide range of topics and called them *Church Dogmatics.* Toward the end of his life, this great thinker was asked if he could make a brief summary of his systematic work. He nodded and answered, "Jesus loves me, this I know, for the Bible tells me so."

That was a huge gift to those of us who bobbed along in the wake of this profound man. Maybe that simple affirmation of faith, coming out of his long view, was the most profound and liberating word of all.

"Jesus loves me, this I know, for the Bible tells me so."

"Do not be afraid . . . it is God's good pleasure to give you the kingdom."

The first year I was the pastor of a church, I was a graduate student in contemporary theology working toward a Ph.D. at Yale. Preaching a sermon every week in my little church turned out to be a more daunting task than the exams and term papers of graduate school. I struggled each week in my first year as a preacher, as I struggled all the years since.

I don't think I could have kept on with being a pastor for long unless I had come across this little prayer by Donald Baillie, a great Scottish theologian and preacher. The prayer is so deeply engraved in my head and my heart that it is part of me, and I call it up and pray it very often:

> Let me no more my comfort draw
>   From my frail hold of Thee;
> In this alone rejoice in awe,
>   Thy mighty grasp of me. [3]

Pray this simple, deep prayer with me, for all our sakes—and the sake of the long view.

~

1.   Dr. Eugene Rosenstock-Huessy, *I Am An Impure Thinker* (Norwich, VT: Argo Books, 1970).

2.   Richard P. Feynman, *The Pleasure of Finding Things Out* (Cambridge, MA: Helix Books, Perseus Publishing, 1999), 255.

3.   D. M. Baillie, *To Whom Shall We Go?* (New York: Charles Scribner's Sons, 1955), 16.

Ted Loder

The Rev. Dr. Theodore W. Loder was the Senior Minister of one of Philadelphia's most unusual churches, the First United Methodist Church of Germantown (FUMCOG), for almost thirty-eight years. With imagination and intensity, Loder led FUMCOG to the forefront of artistic endeavors, political activism, and social justice. His congregation has been a Public Sanctuary Church, a founding church of the Covenant Against Apartheid in South Africa, a Reconciling Congregation that advocates for the rights of homosexual persons.

Loder's own social action grows out of a long history of involvement in social causes, including marching with Dr. Martin Luther King, Jr. in the sixties. Loder is co-founder of Metropolitan Career Center (a job-training program for high school drop-outs); co-founder of Plowshares (a non-profit housing renovation corporation); and co-founder of Urban Resource Development Corporation (an ecumenical effort to rehabilitate abandoned houses). He has also served on the Philadelphia Mayor's Advisory Commission of Children and Families.

For many people who have "given up" on the church, Loder brings a breath of fresh air. His blend of scholarship (cum laude degree from Yale Divinity School, a university fellow of the Yale Graduate School, and two honorary doctorates) and creativity (named by the *National Observer* as "One of America's Outstanding Creative Preachers") stimulate his refreshing openness to hard questions, to change, to relevance, to justice, and to joy.

Dr. Loder currently serves on the National Advisory Board of the National Council of the Churches of Christ in the U.S.A.

More Ted Loder Classics . . .

Guerrillas of Grace
Prayers for the Battle

One of Innisfree's best-sellers! Tough, beautiful earthy prayers. *"These prayers liberate the imagination to new experiences of God, grace, and the stuff of life."—Sojourners*
ISBN 0-931055-04-0 $14.95 Quality Paperback

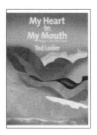

My Heart in My Mouth
Prayers for Our Lives

Gutsy, grace-filled prayers that break out of all formulas. *"Loder's prayers are a lantern to illumine the wonders, terrors, and miracles of our passing days."*—Rev. William Sloane Coffin, Pastor Emeritus, Riverside Church, New York
ISBN 1-880913-49-6 $14.95 Quality Paperback

Wrestling the Light
Ache and Awe in the Human-Divine Struggle

Prayers and stories that reflect the depths and joys of the human struggle. *"If you haven't discovered the contributions of this preacher/poet/ storyteller, let this book be your joy."—Circuit Rider*
ISBN 0-931055-79-2 $14.95 Quality Paperback

Tracks in the Straw
Tales Spun from the Manger

The best of Loder's Christmas stories, with options for advent reading. *"Gives us glimpses of the awesome, startling, and life-changing power of the nativity."—Values & Visions Review*
ISBN 1-8880913-28-1 $12.95 Quality Paperback

Innisfree Press
Visit our website at www.InnisfreePress.com.
Call us at 1-800-367-5872 for a free catalog.
Available from bookstores everywhere.

Innisfree
Press, Inc.
*A call to the
deep heart's core*